MODESTA MATA

NO TO
BULLYING

Ibukku is a self-publishing house. The content of this work is the responsibility of the author and does not necessarily reflect the opinions of the publishing house.

Published by Ibukku.
www.Ibukku.com
Graphic design: Índigo Estudio Gráfico
Copyright © 2018 Modesta Mata
All rights reserved.
ISBN Paperback: 978-1-64086-136-7
ISBN eBook: 978-1-64086-137-4
Library of Congress Control Number: 2018937117

INDEX

The concepts expressed in this book, do not refer to any person, political view, religion, sex, ethnicity, race, city, country, community, or any other created or comparable thing.

Any similarity to a particular fact or situation is only coincidental. It doesn't try to tell parents how to educate their children, but rather; it is the sum of long-standing experience.

Several years working with children and adolescents. It is the result of a free mind that makes use of the freedom granted by free expression and dissemination of thought.

Dedicated to all the victims of Bullying

INTRODUCTION

Bullying at school is the bullying that a victim receives during the school period. Bullying may occur in the classroom, on or off campus. Harassment, bullying, and intimidation, is carried out with the sole purpose of causing annoyance, conscious or unconscious damage. The way to Bully could be quite varied, even so, Bullying is still Bullying. It can be verbal, psychological, with gestures and/or physical when taken to the extreme. The psychological type could be one of the most dangerous because wounds and internal injuries, in most cases, do not heal. Although bullying is usually school-based, there are several places where it can happen. Our purpose is to focus on bullying in schools; children and adolescents will always be our priority.

Bullying in school is a problem that affects and has affected millions of children and adolescents in school, especially when they are in middle and high school.

It is not exclusive to any particular place; this problem has been affecting thousands and countless children and adolescents around the world. Without a way out, and a timely solution so students who suffer day by day and years after years can attend school with peace of mind that they will not be disturbed by other classmates of the same classroom, or the educational center to which they belong, it seems that no solution has been sought to a problem that has taken so many lives. Of course, Bullying in schools has become an obstacle where many kids and adolescents can reach their and their parent's dreams.

It must be recognized that behavioral professionals and counselors working in schools, and other sectors, have been doing and are doing a good job, along with teachers, so both the victim and the perpetrator receive the attention that is required. Despite this hard work, much remains to be done.

This problem of Bullying in school will not be solved until society is involved in the formation and creation of tools and strategies with the purpose of treating and preventing Bullying. Above all, bullying in school is beginning to be seen as a problem which, in one way or another, causes suffering, pain, anguish, despair and is destroying the lives of our greatest treasures; children and adolescents.

A boy, girl or adolescent does not only belong to his family, they belong to all of us as a society, because they are the present and the future; they are the adults and leaders of tomorrow.

Let's focus our gaze on this destructive phenomenon. Let's say Bullying in school, which is not welcome, is a right of children to be able to attend school without fear of being bullied by other students. Educate children and adolescents on the basis of values, love, respect and peace.

BULLYING IN SCHOOL

Bullying in school: it is characterized by the verbal, physical and psychological abuse suffered by some children and adolescents, by one or more classmates in school both inside and out. Children who become victims often do not want to attend school due to the fear of being bullied and/or physically assaulted.

Children who are bullied by a peer sometimes do not dare to tell their parents or guardians. Sometimes because they are threatened by perpetrators and others, for fear of being punished by parents.

Some adults tend to blame them for being assaulted. They assume that they have given some reason. The father with this attitude does not understand that an aggressor does not need a single spark of reason when they want to harass or make someone suffer.

Teenagers are most likely to react with violence and bully another student.

They become violent and aggressive with their classmates in the classroom or school. It is very difficult for a young boy to tolerate any action, even if it is only a gesture. They usually bully someone else who they don't like, for no apparent reason, in the classroom, in the field, cafeteria, or anywhere within their reach during class.

It also happens at school generally, many lurk outside the campuses to attack in group someone they don't like, or for no reason, without measuring their words, or because they don't agree with them. Or even worse, for the simple reason that their friend doesn't like them. For something as simple as not liking someone, they say obscenities and a series of words which are out of proportion and rotten. They attack them physically, verbally and psychologically.

In most cases the perpetrator could be a victim of violence in one way or another, perhaps in their family environment. There are homes that do not use physical abuse in the correction of children and adolescents, but they attack them verbally, causing injuries often incurable, offend them even in front of their friends. In others, they receive threats from an adult who is also a form of violence.

All this is damaging the personality of both young people and children. They reach such a level where their self-esteem is affected. Some are not physically or verbally assaulted.

However, children and adolescents are passively involved in some form of domestic violence by adults and are forced to listen to arguments and fights among themselves, and even witness physical violence among adults; without generalizing. In some homes, they involve them in their conflicts, lawsuits and turn minors into face-to-face participants in the problems between couples, scenes of violence and aggression, whether physical or verbal, the best thing is for them not to take place. If they cannot be avoided; they should be between adults, without children having to be present in these unpleasant situations.

A child or youngster who has had to go through the anguish of watching their mother be verbally and physically assaulted by her partner, and / or husband, who sometimes turns out to be their father, suffer. They tell them so many uncomfortable things to hear that it is also violence towards the child or children; in this case, those who are most affected are the boys and girls. And although it may seem somewhat out of context, or rare, this does not only happen to women, many men are also attacked by women, although perhaps to a lesser extent; in both cases children and adolescents become a kind of recipient that receives the full weight of adult conflicts.

These problems cause children and teenager's desperation, anguish, pain, anxiety, resentment, impotence, an enormous suffering that they need to channel through any means; a situation that affects their behavior, causes them stress, fainting and in the worst of cases they become aggressors of their schoolmates or their own siblings, or displace their anger towards any animal they find in their path. If they do not receive aid at an early age, it will become a vicious cycle, a chain of violence that will continue to be passed down from one generation to the next, it will continue, for a long time to come, it will only change places. Those who fight in front of minors cannot perceive the inner suffering they are leaving behind.

They fight without taking into account they are slowly hurting their children. They do not perceive they are violating their children's rights to live in a peaceful and harmonious home; free from violence.

Everyone must live and grow in an environment of security and tranquility as it corresponds to all children and adolescents in the world. They do not have to be participants or spectators in any kind of violence. These situations are not favorable for their physical and emotional development, but adults must take control of this situation.

If we want good men and women who grow up physically and mentally healthy, it is necessary to provide them with safe environments, where there is no violence of any kind in their presence or against them. It is necessary to create healthy environments that encourage effective communication, where they can express themselves and at the same time feel comfortable.

It is important to search for, find, or take time to talk with children and youth about how school was or some other place where they have gone. Talking to children should be an established rule in the home. Listening to them, attentively. On many occasions, they want to talk to older people, but almost never can. Devoting time to young people and children could free them from future situations that sometimes get out of control. Adolescence is a very difficult time for both young people and adults, but if some measures are taken in the family during childhood, perhaps adolescence would be less catastrophic, traumatic, and chaotic. For some, when children enter their twelfth birthday, they begin to not want to share things with adults unless a very good sense of empathy and trust is created. Above all, young people look for friends and peers to rely on. For some parents, this is something they cannot understand and some handle it calmly while others, become violent and aggressive with their children, worsening the situation.

Young people are going through a transition stage. They, themselves, are facing a real contradiction, their lives are turbulent; they have thousands of questions, without any answers, their body has been changing, their hormones have shot up. They feel like a volcano, but one who does not turn off, even if we let it fall on a river full of water. For teenagers, it's complicated. It's at this stage when complexities come. Some don't like their hands; they are very big or very small. For others, their feet are not perfect, the nose gets a little bulky and they say it's too big. They don't want it like that anymore, they prefer it much thinner. Others don't like their body, and their face is never perfect. It's even worse if they get the so-called blackheads or acne. For everyone, women and men, adolescence is full of a series of problems, which for them and for their parents, become difficult to control. Simply because it's part of the development process of all human beings. It is a bridge we all have to go through to become to adulthood. It is necessary to go through the turbulence of adolescence.

The situation is that some adults have already forgotten that they have passed through this terrible bridge, which has turned out to be more than others, very unstable and shaky. If they thought only a little bit and went back to that time when they were teenagers, they could understand and be able to live with their children in a peaceful and bearable way. Paying attention to your children will not only avoid bad times and stormy moments, but also make it easier for them to cope with the difficulties of this age. When it comes to time and attention, it not about quantity. It is understandable that most people must work in order to meet the needs of daily living.

But that doesn't exempt them from providing quality care for their children. They don't need quantity, but it does mean that they need a few minutes of dedicated quality attention to talk to them and ask them what they did, how their day went, review their homework, help them to do it if they haven't done it, explain to them is not to do it; instead of taking away from them it will add peace of mind to their lives and they will have less headaches.

Young people, and children not only need to be fed with proper nutrition, taken to the doctor to keep them in good physical and mental health, it is very important to pay close attention to their hygiene. Some, when depressed, do not take care of it. Their clothes must be clean and neat, some victims of bullying for this reason.

The adults are the ones who must take control, so they are kept in optimal conditions, not only in the hygiene in all their environment and everything that concerns children so that they have good quality of life and this results in their best interests being met.

Parents cannot be asked to devote all their time to their children because there are many responsibilities of daily living, thousands of commitments and obligations inside and outside their homes, but a minimum of quality time; talking to them, hugging them, observing them, asking them things, supporting them and helping them with their schoolwork, now with great advances in technology, is easier. Even if they do not have an academic education, that is no excuse for not accompanying them during the course of their studies.

There are a million ways to be aware of and accompany them when they do their homework and exercises. You can sit next to them. something that is already help; you can support them, at least by asking them how their day at school was. You have to follow up.

Raising and educating children is the only work in the world that is full-time, overtime, unpaid and long-term. It is twenty-four seven, all night, three hundred and sixty-five days a year; but it must certainly be done with dedication, motivation, and love.

Some children don't speak, especially when something happens to them because of fear and fear of being censored, blamed or punished by adults. Good communication with your sons and daughters would save them immediate suffering and for the rest of their lives. Children will always be children. When given the required attention, teachers and school authorities will have a less complicated job.

All this will be to the benefit of the children and consequently of the parents. Bullying in school is a problem that has not been unique to a certain era.

We do not know when, where and how it began, yet it has made its presence felt, at all times of the school process.

Perhaps, before, it provoked less suffering and pain; it is not a novelty, it affects and has been affecting millions of children and adolescents.

Bullying in school is the constant intimidation and harassment some students receive in school, whose characteristics range from verbal and psychological abuse, gestures, and on various occasions, physical abuse. Sometimes by classmates in the same classroom and so many times outside of it. Sometimes a student in their classroom begins to annoy and intimidate them, or worse, others come and unite to cause suffering to the victim.

If not, they invite others who don't even belong to the school, who only take part because they are friends of a child aggressor. Almost all teenagers take into account the opinions of their friends, they tend to be loyal when it comes to groups or friends, whether they are schoolmates or not. All this happens because they want to show the group that they are strong and courageous, and of course they don't want to be ridiculed in front of their colleagues and friends.

The other problem is that they are influenced by some friends to do certain things, without thinking about the harm they can do to others, nor about the consequences their behavior will bring them and the adults; some never know the things their children do until school calls them. Perhaps because they have to answer for the boy's bad behavior, every action brings a reaction.

If others are assaulted they will be punished in any way, but a teenager never stops to think about consequences. When they are at this age, there is no mind, no time to waste, thinking about what may happen next, and many of them do not care about the consequences. They have reached such a high degree of rebellion, that what they are less interested in are the consequences; depending on how they have been educated, and other times they have received a very good education, the peer pressure is very strong. Sometimes more than their parent's opinions.

However, good communication with children, from an early age, could improve relationships between parents and teenagers so they accept less peer pressure.

Sometimes children begin to be assaulted by other classmates in their classroom, and they don't dare tell their parents, out of fear or poor communication within the family environment. Quality communication with children and adolescents is of paramount importance, because they could trust their parents more than their friends.

Some parents leave their children's education to the entire school system, school, principals, guidance teachers and behavioral professionals. However, family education should fall on parents and guardians. The responsibility and work of the school is academic, rather an integrated work where all parties are involved in different ways. When parents and teachers work together to benefit children and adolescents, parents will have better children and school work will be less complicated and difficult.

The education and training of minors is a continuous task. The future of the country where we have to live by birth, circumstances or because we have chosen to live, for whatever reason, the education of children and adolescents must be a priority.

All of us as a society have the duty to stand up to condemn and say no to violence in all its forms, call it Bullying, which is a violence whose mantle cannot be seen in plain sight, the wounds, even if they are not visible, remain embedded in their thoughts for many years, causing them damage and harming their mental and psychological development.

It is of the utmost importance that special attention be paid to the education and good training of children and young people in households. Something that should not be forgotten is that they will be the doctors, lawyers, accountants, engineers, teachers, nurses, governors, firefighters, leaders, policemen, artists, in general; they will have the command in all the lines, those who today are adults tomorrow will be much older. They will no longer be able to carry out the positions and trades they hold today for various reasons.

However, if appropriate measures are taken to educate boys and girls in less hostile environments, avoiding any focus of violence in front of them, they will be given the opportunity to grow up free, with a clear mind without roots of bitterness and, of course, without prejudice.

Providing them with quality homes, full of peace, regardless of who is the guardian who accompanies them, whether they are their parents by blood or not; Children and young people do not belong only to parents, they belong to society. All of us adults have the obligation and the duty to protect them and work so that they are healthy adults worthy of taking charge of their country. And so that, as they grow and develop, they are able to form homes where aggressions and mistreatment are out of their environment, out of their homes, school and society itself. It is the most appropriate way of forming true citizens; It is the future men and women of today and generations to come.

DYSFUNCTIONAL HOUSEHOLDS

There are millions of households all over the world, from different cultures and backgrounds. Each country has a culture and a very different way of educating its children, some cultures take into account that children and young people follow to the letter the rules, precepts, customs already established, and everything related to their culture. Parents who, regardless of race or nationality, color, religion, social status or other status, want their descendants to be worthy and useful to the society to which they belong.

In almost all families around the world work for the best welfare of their children, not only do they offer them a balanced diet, roofs, clothes, medicine, recreation, affection, good personal hygiene, care, a clean and clean enough home, a good and careful family education, according to their training and culture, all they have learned from their ancestors. Many worry about their children getting a quality education in the different schools where they live or where they live.

They are parents who dedicate themselves to forming good citizens, regardless of whether they have academic formation, or good economic position. The fact is that they have an interest that their descendants have a greater and better quality of life, and that they will be good citizens in the future. People committed to themselves, their children and society, who spare no resources or time as long as their offspring are qualified to live in a changing, globalized and competitive world, where science and technological advances play a very important role, yet not leaving the education of their children in the hands of third parties or of technology.

Committed parents, although they have to work because daily living requires it, and they must exercise their professions or trades, do not neglect their responsibility as parents. Having children is a great commitment. Many people
know that having children is very important, knowing that
you will remain alive through your offspring, when you are
no longer in this world, and with the certainty that you'll
offer individuals with character and good morals to society.
However, exceptions exist. Some children and adolescents
do not receive the treatment they require. They have had to
live in totally unfavorable environments, dysfunctional homes, where they do not receive, or the basics to be able to
develop as healthy individuals and incorporate into society
in a correct way.

When children and adolescents live in stressful homes,
caused by arguments and fights between adults, they can enter
into panic, depression, anxiety, stress and a series of problems
that manifest themselves through shyness, withdrawal. These
could become the victims of other children and adolescents
who manage these conflicts, transforming themselves into aggressors of their classmates or schoolmates.

If adults who fight in front of their children settle their
differences without them being involved in fights and arguments, they would end up less disadvantaged. The best thing
to do would be to wait until your children have fallen asleep
in order to fix their difficulties without the children being
forced to participate in their arguments and quarrels, or rather to look for moments or places where the children are
not present.

Disruptive homes are triggers that lead children to become shy, withdrawn, rebellious or aggressive, and a series of
problems that ultimately complicate the lives of children and
adults alike.

Nonetheless, peace-filled homes where they feel supported and safe could decrease violence among young people.

A home where trust, understanding, responsibility and
respect reign. Someone could say that children should not
have responsibility, when it comes to the responsibilities of
adults like working and fulfilling the duties of older people,
but those who are younger and attending school can take
on the responsibilities of doing schoolwork, and those who
should contribute to making this happen are the parents or
guardians at home. Even if their parents do not know the
language, as if the case when they live in a foreign country.
Even if they haven't had the opportunity to study, they can
help by showing affection and attention. They can do this by
asking how school was or seating by them, even if only for a
few minutes. This will make their children or loved ones feel
like you are giving them attention.

When parents spend a bit of time with their children
when they are younger to do their schoolwork, they feel safer and more enthusiastic about going to school.

Even for teachers the work would be less complicated
if parents and guardians were involved in their children's
homework. For a teacher, it is very painful when children
go to school and enter the classroom without having done
their homework. They already known that something is not
going well at home, it may be something as simple as the
child coming to school without their homework because of
any circumstance.

The problem is when it becomes a habit, it is an indicator that something is happening inside that home or in the
head of that child; the reality is that something we are not
aware of is not working as it should. Motivating children to
do schoolwork is the responsibility of the adults living with

them, whether they are parents or not. But, when discipline in the home becomes very strict, drastic, rigid and unhealthy psychoanalysis can contribute to the deterioration of a child's personality.

They could become submissive or very rebellious. Not only with parents and teachers, but with all those who represent a slight degree of authority. Some will neglect to do their homework, in the case of teenagers it is very likely that they will be taken over by other rebellious youngsters and when the parents come to realize the situation, it is out of their hands. Adults should keep watching their children. Especially when they enter adolescence; this is where their period of rebellion begins. Some neglect their personal hygiene, no longer want to take the bath as it is correct, others neglect to eat or eat out of the ordinary. They talk back and don't want to follow the rules and regulations imposed in the house. In some homes the rules, rules and discipline go beyond the limits, even for an adult to follow them would be quite difficult. There are homes where children and adolescents feel like caged birds, waiting for the minimum second, a minimum gap or space to leave. But such a home is not appropriate for children and young people to grow up in and develop in a healthy, correct and adequate way; physically and mentally.

There are other households that, far from being so rigid, are so flexible that there is no correction of any kind, no rules. The minors can do whatever they want and in their own way without anyone to correct them. So much flexibility ends up being another trigger for inappropriate behavior.

The family that offers an environment of respect with established rules free from violence, children learn to respect people, the rules and norms of society. Especially if they are not just preached; they need adults to be role models. The problem is that each family and each case is different.

There are households where the rules are so rigid that even the grown-ups don't want to submit to them. Parents who are very strict at the end of the day could have some drawbacks.

Children and young people should be offered a place of peace, security, love, harmony, affection, and a certain degree of flexibility, where they can express their feelings, and at the same time be listened to and paid attention when speaking. Some who are victims of Bullying do not dare tell anyone in the house that they are being harassed by other children inside or outside schools. When parents come to find out about this situation, it has already spiraled out of control. Others do not speak because they are threatened by children or teenagers.

Parents who think about their children's well-being watch them, even if they lack time.

Blood-related parents and non-blood related parents are interested in their children being good citizens, but to do this they must work from an early age and on an ongoing basis; without violence, nor retaliation against children.

If a child, regardless of which country or society he or she belongs to, grows up in a household loaded with hostility, where his rights to be children are violated, if assaulted in one way or another, then will become a man or a woman full of resentment, pain, and bitterness. A person whose rebellion will not end even if they obtain all the honors and glory the world could offer...

In order for us to have less hostile adults, it is incumbent on us to do a colossal job. We will have to start at home doing the difficult job of training better men and women, free from hostility, and we will obtain greater benefits by treating them with love, than by verbally offending or beating them.

When you are a child, no one knows, nor do your parents imagine who that child will grow up to be.

With some exceptions, in some cases where parents and teachers recognize talents at an early age, they not only help them to discover these, but support them at all times so that this potential does not remain there as a pearl in the shell at the bottom of the sea, without anyone having the opportunity to enjoy its beauty.

Many children are not so fortunate to have parents with the ability to see their children's skills; or perhaps even if they are able to see the potential, the circumstances of life itself do not allow them to help them unfold from childhood. Only God can see who that girl or boy will be in the future. Others have to wait for him or her to reach adulthood. For that reason, no child should be underestimated, no one knows who he or she will be in the future when they grow up.

Never mistreat an innocent child, because when he grows up he could be your president.

Each parent, depending on the work he or she is willing to do for their child, can more or less determine who their child will be. Sometimes there are uncomfortable situations that are very difficult to resolve, even if they lay the foundations for a good development, it is also not safe because many times parents who have had a great deal of care, dedication and effective work so that their sons and daughters are people of good and useful to society. Young people grow up and create their own destinies given all the teachings their parents and mentors have instilled in them.

Sometimes it is a sort of lottery, but no matter who has decided to have a child, whether they are adults or teenagers, there are many teens who begin to have children at an early age, you must make it your responsibility with dedication and love, knowing that it is not child's play - it is a life. It is a human being who not only needs to be brought into the world, it has to be fed and there are a series of requirements and rules that apply when it comes to be a parent.

In any case, less permissible, hostile, rigid and violent households are more likely to continue this pattern of behavior until they are men and women; and children must be encouraged to resolve conflicts and difficulties through a healthy dialogue free of violence.

To teach rules of adequate coexistence, free from hostility, is the most advisable and convenient thing to do if we want a better future and a society where peace reigns. So, our children and adolescents are able to channel their problems through dialogue, but that is not peppered with any kind of verbal or physical violence, or any kind of psychological intimidation.

The duty of the family and of society as a whole is to form children and adolescents with thoughtful, critical minds who have the freedom to express themselves, without fear of being censored. So, they may carry out their duties and at the same time know and be able to claim their rights without resorting to violence.

Dialogue, diplomatic and passive, will always be the most powerful weapon when seeking a solution to a conflict, or any uncomfortable situation.

A TIME BOMB

When a person hears about a bomb, they are likely to be overwhelmed by fear and panic because, even if it is kept safe and well-guarded, anywhere, in space, at the least expected time it could explode, if the appropriate measures are not taken.

Bullying is a kind of time bomb, which could destroy not only the personality of the victims, even their lives, but also has negative effects for the perpetrator, as well, since their parents will be involved in a situation they must now face.

Without losing sight of the fact that, children and young people who bully others, they themselves have sometimes had to suffer some kind of abuse, violence and/or aggression.

In any case, when they do not receive the care and attention they need, they could become violent by moving around trying to take that aggression to another place, whether they are siblings or classmates or schoolmates.

It may be that some do not actively receive aggression and violence from adults with whom they live in some way; they just participate passively when there are arguments and/ or fights between adults in the home. Other times none of the above happens, however, there is a kind of coldness at home, some distance between adults, the tension takes hold of that environment, which has the same effect on children.

Bullying doesn't start overnight. It's a process that is spreading little by little, without adults noticing it unless children don't have the confidence to talk to them and tell them what's going on.

Perhaps it'd be easier for teachers and professors to notice, but they alone cannot do much. This Bullying problem is complex and very difficult, where everyone should be involved; parents and teachers.

Create solid and lasting strategies to be able to prevent, control and stop, if it is possible to eliminate a problem that ultimately affects us all, even if the children and teenagers are ours, or the society in which we live, today, with the great advances in technology and social networks, we all have the opportunity to find out about everything that is happening around the world, regardless of where on the planet people are located.

Human beings are naturally sensitive, especially when it comes to children and adolescents. In the same way that we rejoice when some of the children or young people perform some feat, a heroic action worthy of being highlighted.

In the same way, when something affects them and causes them sadness or pain, we are also saddened, even if it is not of our family or culture, after all a child is a child, and it is incumbent on all of us to care for and protect it; regardless of race, religion, color or nation to which it belongs. They are all the future of the world. Without children and young people, the human race would become extinct.

Bullying is not just a time bomb that affects the victim, it has serious consequences for the perpetrator. First, because as noted above, they may be victims of some kind of violence themselves.

And because all wrongdoing requires a sanction, where adults will have to be involved and affected, if they are not given the care and supervision they need and deserve. It is a fee that otherwise parents, and society will have to pay.

If we seed a plant of any kind, it can be fruitful, ornamental, big or small, that plant will be as healthy as the one who has planted it allows it to be. And the follow up it receives, everything will depend on what type of fruit, quality and quantity you want to achieve at the end, and as in everything in life, certain rules apply. If you want it big and strong, but do not pay attention and care, its branches will go to the neighbor's land or home.

If you plant one to decorate your garden, without removing weeds or the little plants around it, there will come a time when those you did not plant, will take more strength. It is likely that their growth will be much faster than the one you have planted, and it will naturally end up wrapped by the unwanted, and the good one will turn out to be weak or damaged.

In short, what we are trying to point out is that children as well as plants should not be left to grow without attention, supervision, care and love. If you do not water, clean and remove the weeds that impede it from a good growth and development, it will go crooked. It will dry and/or getting lost in all the bad weeds. The children and young victims of Bullying are sometimes bullied very early in school. Since the beginning of their first years in school and is gradually extended throughout their academic life. Many times, parents are told about the problem, but daily living occupations do not allow them enough time to go to the school to talk with the teacher and administrators about the problem. The other existing problem is that, even if they talk to the teacher, it is not a situation that they as teachers alone can solve. Because young people have their relatives who must be involved in the educational process of their children.

The presence of the parent will always be necessary and important. In another instance, there are more children involved and other parents, who must necessarily be called.

The probability that a parent wants to try to attack aggressive children and young people, could be high. It is very serious error that should never be an option, nor should it be allowed. It never is, nor will it be a good way to resolve a conflict, let alone one between children or adolescents.

Parents should not take violence in their hands against other children or teenagers to defend their own, because in that case, instead of solving the problem, it would take many more complicated paths.

The problems of children and adolescents, when it comes to school bullying, must involve both parents of both children and the education system, in order to find the most appropriate solution for the benefit of the children, both the victim and the perpetrator.

When a child starts refusing to go to school, it is necessary to be alert because unless it is due to another situation outside of school, it could be that he or she is being bullied by other classmates. Children who are victims of Bullying, in addition to not wanting to attend school, are gradually lowering their grades and this is an indicator, so parents and teachers can realize that something is not going well. If there are no problems inside the home, that could be the cause of the problem.

If not, it is up to the school to investigate whether the child's behavior is caused by problems at home.

Some children are a bit burdensome at school, but with very good motivation from parents and guardians, or whoever is in charge of them, they could change their behavior, as well as many teachers who are quite motivating and make the classroom a pleasant place for children where they feel comfortable.

Compassion between students and teachers could help keep children motivated, enthusiastic and eager to go to school. It is very important to look for strategies within the classroom so that they can meet all the expectations of the teaching and learning process and not feel discouraged and bored.

It's not to say the classroom should be made into a playground, but just a place where children can feel relaxed, at ease and do their homework in and out of the classroom. A child who is enthusiastic in school will be a child who, upon arriving home, will do all the homework and chores assigned by the teacher.

When children and young people are not comfortable for one reason or another, they may not feel motivated to do homework assignments given by the teacher. When some parents leave all of their children's work and responsibilities to schools and teachers, move a step forward by changing their minds, believing that teachers have a magic wand that must work for children, as well as learning to maintain excellent behavior, within the classroom and on campus. Good reasoning, in favor of working together as a whole, to maintain constant communication with the children's teachers and professors, to know how they are responding academically, and how they behave in school.

I have met some parents who register their children in schools, and after that they never ask again how the student is responding to it. Whether they are a child or an adolescent, it is a duty and a right of parents to keep abreast of the learning process. Other parents do not attend school meetings, which is a good opportunity to learn about their children's academic progress and behavior.

Parents who maintain contact and good relationships with their children's educators have a greater impact on both their grades and the way they behave; it becomes a joint duty. These same parents, are the ones who pay attention to the children's homework by helping and supporting them, even if it is just through being present at the time to do them. Both the school community and the parents can set the quota that corresponds to each one, so that that time bomb that is Bullying does not reach any home, nor the schools. And, in case it arrives, it should not be on hold until it expands and ends up destroying some life. Before this happened, they must put on the corrective measures it deserves in each case; because each one is different, just like the circumstances that gave rise to the same.

There is a high probability that this Bullying problem will be solved. For something like this to happen, society must be united, to work against Bullying, never, never, ever against the perpetrator, a bullying child or adolescent in need of help, both from relatives and from school.

With the certainty and security that true education does not come from school, it has its roots in the home.

When parents and teachers work together, parents and teachers will have a better future for their children.

BULLYING AT HOME

All the time there has been talk of bullying at school, psychological cyber-bullying, but the silent, masked, destructive and harmful bullying of which some children are victims within their own home, has never been considered.

While focusing on the fact that in most cases it is mostly parents and close relatives, this is not at all premeditated, much less for the purpose of hurting or injuring children and adolescents, it is a bullying that may not have a premeditated intention, it is not like school bullying that intends to assault the victim.

This bullying, even if it is not intentional and premeditated, is a double-edged sword and above all dangerous weapon, which can end slowly, destroying, and minimizing the personality of children to lower their esteem; leaving them vulnerable to any later uncomfortable situation that may arise, regardless of whether it is intentional or not.

Their feelings are being wounded, hurt, in the end it all turns into resentments against adults.

Sometimes an angry parent uses children as a dart against another adult. Whoever does that is not thinking about the harm they are doing to their son or daughter. When an adult is assaulted through children or adolescents, the esteem, character and personality of these children and adolescents is being destroyed.

They are not matured enough to receive such attacks. Children become recipients in which some individuals deposit all the resentment and anger they have against the other adult.

It hurts children when they say something against one of their parents. Even if they aren't perfect, every child in the world deserves to have parents who are committed, protective, kind, caring, affectionate and good; children don't choose their parents.

Some children receive bullying inside their own home, even if they do not intend to attack. It leaves indelible traces on the children, but the adult does not stop to think about the wounds it leaves, let alone that it is destroying the child's life.

Some would say they do it unconsciously, but if it is unconscious, it is not a problem. It could be that there is no intention to harm, yet all the bullying is to the detriment of the children and as a drop of water falling on a stone, is going to slowly destroy its personality slowly; it will crumble its character.

Psychological aggressions are serious and harmful for children. When they are adolescents, the damage is deeper, they are in the most vulnerable stage of human development. They are trying to find themselves, since when they look in the mirror, they are not children or adults.

This state of turbulence, vulnerability, and inconstancy does not offer them security. If they do not find it inside their home, in the bosom of their family, they will go in search of it, outside with their friends.

When young people do not find support at home, they will look elsewhere for it. In the end, parents end up being harmed because regardless of whether or not they are good, they are still their children. It is not something that can be changed, even if people give their child up for adoption, nothing will change that biological process; it will not prevent them from carrying their blood and remain their child.

Bullying in the home: it is the most destructive of all but has never been paid attention to. No one recognizes it as such. Bullying in disguise has been present in some homes of our society. Without attention being paid to it or looking at it as a problem that spreads; taking its branches to other places, especially to school, in addition to hurting the individual from an early age, causes affliction, grief, suffering. Sometimes the children are distressed, saddened, upset and the adults who live with them cannot imagine what they are going through. But hurtful words end up consuming minors, some become very submissive. Others, violent, aggressive, aggressions that can get out of the house and go to school, against other children if the situation was complicated in their family environment. When it goes beyond school or the classroom, it becomes even worse.

In some homes, they start by naming the child after themselves. Once I hear a mother telling her newborn baby, what do you want with your toad eyes? He was crying a lot, something was happening to him. When babies cry they are transmitting a message that the mother may not understand at that moment. She told him so, because he had quite big eyes, to another mother who had just given birth and I went to visit at the hospital. She had given birth to a boy, she said to me; he is ugly, has a mouth like a door, he had a big mouth. I told her no baby is ugly, and everyone comes with its own mouth. These were newborn babies who still didn't understand anything about the situation that was happening around them, let's just imagine that the inappropriate behavior of these two mothers will continue throughout the child's life.

Many times, they tell children lots of horrible things, from rotten words to insults. Instead of calling them by their own names, they tell them unimaginable things. If they are thin they bully them for being thin, tall or short, they bully them anyway, because of their skin color, they bully them by the nose, their hands, and with all the body parts of the children.

All that happens in some homes. This instant is the precise moment, the exact hour, to stop this situation. That action that some relatives have of bullying children from an early age is not a school problem; that verbal and psychological violence does not have roots in any school. Its origin is in other places, far away from it, yet it arrives there because the children must necessarily attend an educational center. But they are not all child victims or perpetrators. This assures us that not everything is lost, most of the children who attend school maintain optimal behavior, it is only a small minority who become victims and perpetrators.

This reveals to us that there are reasons and causes for some children and adolescents to bully others. Our job must be to look for them, treat them, apply the necessary treatment to eliminate them. There must be some solution; those who receive support, safety, affection, protection and care are less likely to tease others at school.

We need to raise awareness in families, to offer violence-free homes and society itself must play its part; no child or adolescent should ever receive any aggression of such magnitude, because to those who do not perceive that they are tearing their world apart; the future of children and society is being affected by the bulling at home.

Children who are bullied at home are almost always depressed, troubled, discouraged, disappointed, disillusioned, apathetic, lacking optimism, are pessimistic children, everyone finds them negative. Their world becomes dark, not only is Bullying, which is violence, able to hide well behind any cloak, they are sometimes exposed to all kinds of violence. Even if it is not recognized that children are bullied in their family environment, it is causing them su-ffering that causes behavioral change. In order to prevent, stop bullying at school, the first and most important step is to stop bullying towards children at home; whether conscious or unconscious, it is equally harmful to them. It's not that in every home they bully children, no, but there are families who bully them, and their personality worsens, causing them low esteem and a series of emotional problems that they may not be able to heal.

A family member who assaults the child probably won't stop to think for a second about the harm he or she is causing, or even how extensive the impact on his or her behavior will be. But the child who feels assaulted will no longer be as ha-ppy and cheerful as every child should be. It is important to let them enjoy their childhood, games and fun at that age. Emo-tionally assaulted children, begin to feel that they are not so pretty, beautiful, when they notice their imperfections. More in the case of females who look in the mirror, if they are told that their eyes are beautiful, that's what they will believe, but if they are told that their hands are too big, imagine how he or she will feel. Maybe you don't want to go to school with the same enthusiasm that you did before. Even if your little hands aren't so big, you will see them gigantic. The things that are said to them have a great impact on their thinking, their minds and their daily lives. But especially in their future, whatever you tell them, remember that your child will be tomorrow what you tell them today; they begin to form at a young age. Is a kind of foundation like when the builders are going to make a big building; the size, strength and its duration will depend on how big and strong the foundation is, nothing can be built, where there isn't a good base. In the end, a weak breeze will be enough to damage it. The child victim of Bullying, no ma-tter where he or she is being assaulted, in the end, his or her esteem will be weakened in one way or another. Sometimes they do not want to attend school, or end up with inappropriate conduct, and/or ultimately, they may become abusers of other children or adolescents. Great care must be taken with what we plant in the minds of children, lets plan in them values, positivism, push them to sound, to succeed, but the adults are the role models. It is important that they build homes full of harmony, peace, security, love, patience. To raise children, tolerance, love and dedication is required. Let's eradicate from homes, physical and emotional abuse. Bullying only harms them, drags them into making mistakes and a series of triggers that lead the boys to get involved in situations from which they ultimately find no way out. The person who does not act correctly by treating children well is weakening their personality. Is leading them into a maze that may eventually find no way out. Once the Bullying originated innocently at home, it will not stop it from going to other places, to school in particular. It is time to stop bullying by not letting it occur at its source, and if it is its sacred nest, many more, homes and schools must be places where children and adolescents feel safe, comfortable, respected and protected. Adults must serve as role models. Although many adults don't stop to think, children are little judges, who realize what all the people who were born before them do, not only to observe the behavioral patterns of grown-ups, but to draw their own conclusions, without anyone telling them their analysis of what's right and wrong. Knowing that they will be the adults of tomorrow, it is better that we treat them, both properly and at the same time be their role models. Adults are now the developers, builders, and leaders of society. Let us form good builders so this building, called "world where we are all tenants", has more and more capable men and women, physically and emotionally healthy. Always remembering that true education is not born in school, it has its roots in the home.

There is no better school for children than the one you can find in your family environment. The house is and should be their main school, a good family education is essential for their good behavior and development in society. This does not mean that you will leave your child at home to educate them, academically, without seeing the sunlight and without them being able to share with other children. No, that's not the message, quite the opposite. The aim is to have more healthy children, who are not victims or bullying perpetrators anywhere in the world.

Children from an early age should socialize, relate to others in their environment or schools so that they can grow, learn and develop normally.

The aim is to ensure that children and adolescents grow up in a good home where they are not attacked, with no violence, active or passive. May society itself provide a safe platform where everyone can live in harmony and peace. Stopping all forms of bullying from starting at home is the first step and the best way to prevent and stop bullying at school. All of them deserve to be helped to grow up healthy in every sense of the word, not to hurt their feelings, to have their rights respected and to be taught their duties, but with love, even though they are teenagers, they have not finished developing, neither physically, nor mentally. they need unconditional support from adults to continue on the path of life.

It has not yet been created, nor will there ever be a weapon more powerful than love.

All of us, without exception, must be aware of the need to educate our children and adolescents without mistreatment or abuse, without any kind of violence inside or outside their homes, causing them suffering, pain and anguish.

It is true that they need to be disciplined, rather than disciplined, they need good guidance to be guided in the right direction; but NOTE, without hitting, hurtful, upsetting, or humiliating words; without gestures that in one way or another manifest aggression.

Some people, without thinking about the harm they do to children, from a very young age tell them they are useless. They are planting erroneous information about them in their mind, which will eventually deteriorate their character and personality. They will believe that which they have been told so often is true. Anger growing in their mind, like a seed of weed until it has coupled their whole being, inside and out. When they reach adolescence, it becomes very difficult for them to change and specially if, in the process, they do not find a behavioral professional, psychologist or psychologist to help them with good treatment. Changing that way of thinking and tearing out all the words that have sown in their little head. They'll always believe that word they heard about themselves. Another word often used by adults against children is: you are stupid. No child is stupid, even though they are small, they have wisdom and intelligence, sometimes much higher than some adults.

That's not a proper way to treat minors. They deserve to be spoken to without mistreatment; the offensive words must be stopped. No abuse of any kind serves to make the children and adolescents more obedient or calmer, on the contrary, attacking them will only encourage them a kind of internal rebellion, which in addition to lowering their esteem will deteriorate their personality. Or they become withdrawn and shy and/or on the contrary, very rebellious and spiteful.

Children who are not treated with affection and respect will create a layer of resentment in their minds and inner selves. Accompanied by roots of bitterness that sooner or later harmed their lives and those of their parents. Previously, and still today, there were and still are homes that continue to correct children with a series of verbal and psychological abuse, and in some cases even physical abuse.

Practice that must change as that way of disciplining creates anxiety and stress; depression. Emotional blows never heal, those scars can't be seen. But they are as severe as those left by physical shocks and at the same time trigger a series of psychological illnesses that could turn into physical and mental pathologies. A sad, anxious, fearful, shy or rebellious child, will be a child who will make very little progress in school, and in his or her social relationships, will become distracted, and/or disinterested, who will not want to attend school. And if they attend, they will be afraid to return home with fear of being mistreated. Children who are not comfortable at home become vulnerable to other, much more dangerous situations. Many children and adolescents not only drop out of school, but also leave their homes to flee the abuse they receive where they are supposed to be protected and treated well. Perhaps it is a practice that, as passed down from generation to generation in some families, adults never think they are harming children.

It's never too late to change a practice that far from fixing children's problems for the rest of their lives. It is necessary to change abuse and mistreatment for affections, and to find the right way to train future leaders and rulers of society. it is necessary to remember that they will not always be children, just as they will grow up, it is better to treat them well.

If we lose our sanity, when it comes to correcting and disciplining them, if we let fury, anger, and/or rage blind us, we could end up hurting them with words, or physically. Whoever the adult is, in one way or another, will pay some kind of dues. Abuse is not just beating or assaulting them verbally. Not taking them to the doctor, caring for them when they get sick, or not giving them their medicine in time, not providing adequate nutrition, is also abuse. Letting others assault or violate their rights, neglect of personal hygiene, keeping them in an unhygienic home, not treating them with respect is also abuse.

Denying them affection and affection, marginalizing them, leaving them abandoned or in the hands of people who do not provide good care. People who may attack them or harm them in any way, becomes mistreatment. A series of behaviors that for some adults go unnoticed, but in short, harm minors in one way or another. Until all these household misbehaviors are corrected, school bullying will not stop.

Aggression against children and adolescents can come in any form and from different people. Ignoring and neglecting them is another form of abuse that can make them resentful and rebellious, tipping the scales to one side, paying more attention to one in the presence of the other child, is already affecting their rights. It is not fair to compare them to anyone else. Comparisons between one and the other lead nowhere. Each person is unique and different, no child has to be a faithful copy of the other, even if they are siblings or parents. If we look at the fingers of the hands and observe them carefully, we can see that they are all different. People are unique, children and adolescents are different, even if they are siblings or from the same family. Today is precisely the time, the day and the hour to stop comparing them with someone, everyone is unique and unrepeatable, comparisons also become aggressions.

When the aggressions against children and adolescents stops at home, we will be taking the first step on the immense staircase which is needed to stop bullying in schools and every other form of bullying. An education based on healthy dialogue. a home where their rights are respected, where peace and harmony reign, where the elderly discuss their differences in private. Not to make their children participate in their "he said she said". Not involving children in their dissatisfaction, problems, conflicts and arguments will be best for everyone. Let minors have freedom of thought and speech, with their parents expressing themselves without being censured. There are many homes around the world that provide environments full of freedom, love, quietness and well-being for their children. Although it is true that in others it is not the case. It has nothing to do with whether those who have such a great responsibility to care for children and adolescents are surrogate parents or those who have conceived them. In short, they are parents, and they must meet their needs as it is right, with love and tenderness, without having to impose straitjackets on them. Children need homes that meet their needs.

At least the basic ones, such as food, education, health, recreation, and affection. And to help them grow up mentally and physically healthy and where they have the trust to share things with their parents or relatives. Everything that may be happening to them or simply telling them how their day was at school, or perhaps where they went. It will work better than creating a hostile environment where they become suspicious of adults.

No wary child or teenager can be happy and, even less, able to maintain sufficient concentration at school. All of us, without exception, must unite our efforts and all that is within our reach. Let us join our voices so that all children live in homes where they are treated with dignity, allowed to develop normally, in a healthy way. That is the formula for a better society, and to stop bullying in school.

All adults today have the power to change the world for today's children and future generations.

If we start in the homes with a good family upbringing, based on respect, it could become an effective tool. Above all, a good and effective medicine for the prevention of bullying. They will be able to attend every day of their lives the best school ever. However, if the family does not participate in their family and academic education, the teachers' work will not be lost, and it would be more difficult.

The family is, and will continue to be, the main focus of children's education.

The family is the main society, let us all form a better, safer and much more secure world for present and future generations. Let us all fight together for children and adolescents against bullying. Not against the perpetrator, nothing will be achieved by judging him or her, as long as the roots that lead him or her to cause emotional and physical injury to others are not eliminated.

Prevention plays a decisive role in any situation.

Let's start at home to prevent bullying at school.

ENABLING ENVIRONMENT

The vast majority of parents, regardless of whether their children are adoptive, birth or foster parents, recognize that raising children is a great responsibility and a huge task. It is a full-time, long-term, commendable job that deserves to be followed up, whose only payment is to see your children grow up healthy, fulfilled and happy. Although usually full of joy, sometimes pleasantness and sadness cross each other, even when parents do everything right so that everything related to their children works in the best possible way. Almost everyone who has had and is privileged to have children. seek to give them a dignified life, create the most favorable, adequate and healthy environment within their reach, with or without knowledge, that the environment in which children grow up has much to do with their later development, when they are adults. With its rare exceptions, a home where children can express themselves freely, homes with effective communication, parents concerned about their children's best welfare; have more opportunities.

To provide a better future for them, both personal and academic, the children who receive the support of their closest relatives. Whether parents or not, the most important thing is for children to be able to live and grow up in environments that are conducive to their physical, mental and psychological development. Especially in the early years of their lives that are decisive for their development and their unfolding in society. A good foundation in their early years will be a very good platform for them to increase their intellectual and physical development. A child can come gifted to be a genius, but if you don't find a home that will provide you with the tools to develop all that capacity you were endowed with, your gifts and skills may not be able to achieve the development you require for that potential to reach its maximum expression. Even those with normal aptitudes, intelligence and potential, like most people, need homes that provide them with all the necessary and adequate elements to grow and develop properly. Those who are below average, if they have the privilege and opportunity to be born and grow up where they are offered proper attention in the full sense of the words that children require, will achieve a great development in their adult life. All children need affection, care, protection, adequate nutrition according to their age, medical attention, and support in their schoolwork when they are in school. The likelihood of reaching adolescence without dropping out of school will be higher and higher than those who do not receive by right all that children deserve just because they are children. Unfortunately, there are a number of cases that do not receive even the slightest bit of favorable conditions. The rights, they as children, should receive regardless of their social status, race, color, any other status or society in which they are born, raised and developed. A child is a child. There is no treasure that has as much value as children. For this reason, there are inalienable rights that are specific to this stage of life, and they should not be violated under any circumstances, nor under any pretext.

Of course, they also have certain duties which adults should gradually teach them according to their age. One of their greatest duties is undoubtedly to attend school from their early years, so that they begin to socialize with other children. This is how they learn, and their mental development will become stronger every day. The more they socialize, the stronger their mental strength, the more self-esteem they build as they learn. It is a set of those who learn from the environment at home and in school with other children because everyone has different experiences. In each house the lifestyle is different, that varied learning will foster a high degree of socialization that at the same time will offer the necessary tools for their personal growth; so, when small difficulties, differences and conflicts with one or another peer come, their mind and self-esteem will be forged. Little by little, both in their family environment and in the process of socializing with friends and siblings, when they are there to help them in all their development, it is of paramount importance to strengthen their mind, their self-esteem.

In such a way that he or she has a sustainable psychological level that allows them to endure the aggressions without being psychologically affected, and that they have the confidence to tell their teachers that at that moment they are the closest people they have. And, in the same way, they can communicate with their parents and guardians to let them know they are being verbally assaulted. This being the case, there is a much greater chance that problems between children will be resolved in time, before they become physical violence. Our intention is, prevention first of all, and then for Bullying to be eradicated in all its aspects, but we must not forget that we live in a world where everyone has different experiences and therefore a different history. Since there are variables that may not be fully controlled, children need to learn to live with the difficulties that arise in the lives of all humans. It is necessary that they are mature and strong enough to be able to withstand any conflict. Problems will come, in one way or another, but must affect them as little as possible.

A first step could be to work on children's self-esteem from infancy, so that they can live in a world where they will find all sorts of choices. Everyone is different and behaves in the way they have learned from the environment in which they have developed with a few exceptions. Many schools work on children's self-esteem in one way or another. In reality, that's a job your family definitely has to do. It is in the home that the esteem of infants should be encouraged. To speak to them according to their age, strengthen their mind. Let them know how valuable and important they are to their family and society.

Without going beyond limits, they need to know that they are loved. Some think they are not wanted, and that's already a big problem. Let children know that their parents and closest relatives love them regardless of their condition, that they are wanted. Kids aren't foolish as some people think or believe. Even when they are small, they perceive who offers them good treatment and protects them; sometimes they have doubts. You have to strengthen any emotional weakness and answer their questions, which should be answered according to their age. As children grow older, they have their observations, questions and answers, their own analysis, so don't lie to them, or extend beyond what they want to know.

If you don't give them the correct, accurate and adequate answers, they will go to school with their classmates, cousins, neighbors, television and especially in social networks when they are a certain age. The environment in which children operate is very important when faced with conflict, at school or elsewhere. It is not the same thing, a child who is being victimized by Bullying, who comes from a family that has supported and nurtured their courage. Their esteem, their reaction will be very different from that of other children who have not found trust, affection, care, protection and above all good communication at home. The first society, the primary one, and the most important and at the same time determining in the future life of the children, is their home.

Society must provide them with the main tools so that they are able to cope with the various difficulties that one way or another arise in people's lives. In this world, we all live. we can't expect everyone to behave in the same way. In every household, there is a different society with knowledgeable customs and cultures that are as variable as people exist. Children are going to face very different problems. We cannot isolate them, place them far from the things that are part of everyday life. The only thing we can do is to create a very good platform, a proper foundation for them as children to learn to live in a competitive world, where besides all the wonderful good things it has, there are also circumstances where difficulties arise. When you have worked on their mental strength, their self-esteem, it will help them when those hurricane winds rise mercilessly. Call it Bullying or any other problem they may have.

Do not make the mistake of not sending children to school or letting them communicate with other children in their environment or school. Let us imagine that we plant two little plants of the same species. One, we leave enclosed, without the light, the heat of the sun, the rain falling, the breeze and the wind whipping when it arrives with its implacable fury, without it receiving the serene of the night and the morning dew. And the other that on the contrary remains exposed to all of the above. What has been present in all these difficulties of life will grow stronger and more likely to survive, even when the strong winds come. Because it's grown strong, it has more stamina. It is not intended to make comparisons between children and a little plant, it's just a simple example. In general terms, children who develop in a healthier and more appropriate environment, who socialize with others, who are learning that in life there are difficulties, and who must know how to get out of them without being harmed, and without causing any harm to anyone. It may not be possible to control that children are victims of bullying. They are not going to be placed in a glass box either, but they can be formed so that they can live without being so vulnerable, when someone bullies them. Let them know that they are valuable, important, and can count on their relatives at every moment, place and space wherever they go. Households that teach children that there are many people in the world and that each of them has different tastes, opinions and preferences, different ways of thinking and seeing things. And, that the ways of others must be respected; even if one does not agree, or does not like it, everyone has the right to think and do as they please as long as their behavior does not cause others harm; without getting bullied.

Children must learn not only to respect the rights of others, to demand their own rights, but to be free from violence. Bullying is a kind of violence. Only that it hides behind any cloak, which sooner or later unleashes serious consequences for the victim and of course for the perpetrator as well. But, who ends up losing at the end of the day, is the victim who may not be able to bear the suffering and situations left behind by the aggressions. The family plays a vital role in the development and development of children. Parents and guardians who are involved in the education, training and development of their children in order to prepare them for the future by building a dignified life for them and strengthening their self-esteem. giving them the right and opportunity to interact with other children and teenagers in an atmosphere of peace, solidarity, tolerance, respect. Where education is to integrate with a strong emphasis on emotional and psychological issues. Teaching them that even if they live in a world that could become violent, violence is not the best way to fix any setbacks along the way. Dialogue, peace, and countless options exist in life to settle disagreements without resorting to violent means. At first the Bullying is a passive violence, it begins with subtle words, other hurtful ones, with gestures, which in the end, can turn into physical violence. There comes a time when things get out of control and turn into more than words, pushes and blows appear on the scene. The point is not to teach them to bear and let themselves be harassed much less hurt. This cannot and will not be the solution, the aim is that children can live in an environment without violence of any kind, that, if someone tries to attack them, they do not respond with violence, because with violence nothing is achieved. Children are entitled to live in places where peace and harmony are fostered, especially when they are in school.

Much of their lives and lives are spent in school. Some children may not attend school due to circumstances beyond their control. But it's normal for all children to go to school to prepare for adulthood. It's everyone's right, without exception. If we train them to use appropriate means, tell their teachers if they are in school and have enough confidence with their parents or guardians to find the best way to resolve the problem before someone ends up being harmed. The support that parents provide for their children is invaluable in their physical, psychological and intellectual development. All of this will have repercussions throughout their lives and over the years. Let's begin to create homes that will ultimately favor the good coexistence of all minors, remembering that tomorrow they will be adults, parents and guardians, technicians, teachers, presidents, governors and will be performing each and every one of the functions and offices that adults perform. They will be the leaders. Supplying, building, providing and facilitating healthy, welcoming, adequate and favorable homes is always, and should be the responsibility of parents and guardians. Without neglecting all the support that school and society should provide and can do for children.

CYBER BULLYING

Cyber bullying is the harassment of a person through so-cial networks, with the intention of causing serious da-mage to the individual's character; Without thinking about the terrible emotional and psychological consequences they would cause for the victims.

Bullying is so common, harmful, perverse, destructive, and long-lasting. Bullying by means of networks, not only has the purpose of attacking, it goes further. It is intended, in addition to assaulting the victim, for the purpose of disclosing; letting everyone know. That's when his or her sickness is satisfied, what makes this category of bullying a high-risk, dangerous, unhealthy aggression, the mockery and shame that suffer the majority of victims, generates sadness, anxiety, anguish, depression and a series of psychological symptoms triggered when the victims are assaulted via social media, or through any channel. Feeling assaulted in public is so damaging that some victims of Bullying have ended their lives. Leaving their families with irreparable loss and sorrow. Although Bullying is suffered by children and adolescents in schools, in social media bullying extends beyond childhood and adolescence, in this case although it is true that the majority are adolescents, some adults are also victims of Bullying.

Many people tend to do bullying, even in their own family, in order to attack them with words. Family members who bully children may not understand that they are being harmed. Their character slowly deteriorates. The problem is that not everyone is so mentally and psychologically strong to endure and to put on the mockery that someone with little human sensitivity gives them. Something as unpleasant as bullying should be seen as a matter that undoubtedly causes pain in people, is inhumane because it injures and attacks the tranquility and emotional stability of the victim. In recent times, Bullying has gained a high profile. People engaged in this type of activity are very likely to never measure the consequences and difficulties they cause their victims. Use some social media to violate and disrupt the tranquility and peace of others rather than use it to do productive or positive things as thousands and millions of people around the world do. Social networks are outstandingly good, and they have contributed to globalizing the world, saving lives, bringing families together, getting friends, keeping society informed, saving time, money; closing the gap. It not only unites people, families, but also keeps us together and connected. They also serve as a link between peoples and nations, and even in the most distant places of the world, they have the opportunity to be informed through these networks. They are an excellent means of communication. They have united the world and people no matter what corner of the planet they are in. They are one of the most important things that have been created in the world. However, cyberbullying has become a problem, a real-world nightmare. How many young men, women and adults, regardless of their sex or orientation, have had to suffer for the monster of cyber bullying. Whole families who have had to endure the tempest of seeing their loved ones suffer depression, sadness, pain, anxiety, and suffering from a series of post-traumatic psychological symptoms. Those who have been assaulted by other people, embarrassing them, even for reasons that at a given moment are beyond their control. There are so many variants that it is not possible to control them in the life of some people.

People, situations of suffering and pain and if you add to that the ghost of cyber-bullying whoever it is, no matter how strong it may seem, if you bully them for something that has gone out of their control, is condemned to despair. Giving them unnecessary discomfort, leading them to the extreme decision to attempt their own lives, as its happened many times before.

In addition to the victim, their relatives suffer, society is affected, and everyone in general. a whole conglomerate of people around the world has been harmed because everyone wants to or doesn't end up knowing what happened. Bullying is destructive, isolates its victim from society, slowly diminishes its character and its personality is deteriorating. Perpetrators may not be able to understand the complexity of the upcoming problem at this time. Bullying not only deteriorates, it also acts as an obstacle for people who are assaulted to progress in their daily lives as well as in the professional environment. The torture suffered by people robs them of all the desire to go on with a normal life like everyone else. Because it is complex and complicated, it is necessary to look for urgent solutions, create tools and strategies in order to prevent, stop, eliminate and eradicate bullying in all its aspects.

This silent, masked enemy is far more serious than any disease, devastating, corroding and destroying or perhaps more harmful than some of those storms that strike. A child or young person who is bullied, does not manage to have peace, is tormented, causes confusion, disturbance creating in the person an emotional imbalance that does not let him or her sleep, or live in freedom; a situation that must change. Bullying is more dangerous than any disease, it attacks its victims, ending the existence of human life. In other cases, the victims end up mutilated psychologically, they cannot recover from this problem. This ghost haunts them everywhere. It's time to look for forms, ways and strategies at the social level, creating educational tools that raise awareness to give a resounding NO to cyber bullying or by whatever means. At school, on the street, at work, at home, it is a problem that loses out, and affects other people, the family and society as a whole. Every human being has the right to live in our society without the need to be assaulted, mocked, harassed, with or without cause, there is no valid reason for a person to have to receive suffering. At the end of the road, the same thing happens to everyone, as a human race, why attack each other?

There is no reason for a family to see one of its members suffer from bullying. Whoever does the bullying is forgetting something very important; they are also human beings. The human race has only one code. As such, is exposed to the same things happening to them. Why not use social networks for all those good and fabulous things which they were and have been created for instead of using them to cause suffering and hurt an individual and families with bullying. Whoever does such a thing think that they are harming only one person, yet it is attacking a society.

No one lives alone in the world, not even animals. Most species need to live in a community, even plants. We all form the planet. the universe is made up of all that is in it and those who inhabit it, the water, the earth, we are all part of a totality. Birds, even the smallest particle, the same universe claims the harmony of all living beings that inhabit it. It is not necessary to make someone suffer, making them suffer, perhaps at that moment they might be going through difficult times. Many people have situations and circumstances that cause them pain and sadness, if you add more pain to that, the person will end up displaced or submerged in a maze they may not be able to leave.

Bullying ends with the esteem and personality of other people directly or indirectly. Even if the person suffering from bullying does not belong to his or her race, country, community, social status, religion or anything else in particular affects us all. It is important to think that it is a problem, that besides bringing terrible consequences, it will not be easy to get out of this problem. It is convenient to think of others, theirs could be wounded, take the fruits of that which has been sown, this is how the law of the universe works.

It receives as much or more, in the measure it gives. It is easier to make someone happy than to harm them, so they suffer. Highlighting people's positive qualities is characteristic of self-confident, self-satisfied and highly esteemed people. Families have a hard time seeing one of their own growing up in every aspect, as if they had to suffer because someone destroys everything they have done over time so their relative is in optimum condition to be a good person. It is not at all flattering to observe how their efforts are broken and destroyed because someone cold, calculating and ruthless is pleased having fun at the expense of inflicting pain on others. To stop this evil which, while it is true that it may not directly affect, in one way or another hurt and destroys. Better and more effective work would be done if, instead of hurting, the achievements and qualities of others were highlighted. Honoring and emphasizing others, dignifies and enhances.

As other people do, they are responsible for highlighting the qualities that others in the world possess. They highlight the good and positive things they do. It is time to think and stop all kinds of Bullying, most people who are victims of Bullying end up isolating themselves from others and society. In most cases they cause irreparable damage in one way or another. A person who has been a victim of Bullying gets depressed, doesn't want to have friends, go out and have fun, doesn't want to do everything they did before feeling attacked by Bullying. some close themselves in, others fall into a much more dangerous abyss. No family should ever lose a member to Bullying.

Perhaps anyone who provokes a tragedy by bullying does not do so thinking that the situation would get out of control, causing extreme harm. The fact is that many people have succumbed, and others have not succeeded in overcoming this cause and it is time to stop this practice which, far from doing well or benefiting someone, causes pain, sadness and bitterness to the victims and their families. This Bullying behavior is unacceptable and cannot be continued as mere spectators watching as children, youth and adults are emotionally disabled. Society itself should not stand back and watch out for bullying to follow different people. we must join forces to stop all Bullying behavior. It is not that actions are taken against people, but rather, it is creating tools to prevent and stop behavior. To develop educational campaigns, both for families and schools, in favor of the physical safety and emotional stability of adolescent children. Education is the most powerful weapon in ending any situation, however complicated it may seem. It is very likely that the same people who do the bullying, do not measure the magnitude of the problem that is coming as a result of their behavior. the same aggressor inside must feel some kind of feeling of guilt, being forced to think that it should not incur in such action where innocent people are affected. Some people may think that it is impossible for cyberbullying to stop, or anyone else because there will always be people who want to use these or other means to harm others. But not everything is lost. At this moment in time when I am embodying these lines I do not know if there are laws, to sanction those who engage in cyber bullying for having caused psychological harm and / or push someone to cause themselves harm. Not only the individual, but also families and society. Cyber-bullying should be treated as a crime, so victims should be compensated by those responsible for this behavior, for bullying someone. Not only should victims receive treatment paid for by the perpetrators if they are adults and if minors are responsible for them, they should compensate both victims and their families in the event of a loss of the person. Deaths from this type of behavior, which can disappear if taken to the same extent and with the same impact on victims, families and society, cannot continue. Nothing is impossible. Bullying can be eradicated in all its aspects. As long as there is the provision, that all people reject this conduct, not the person. Rather the behavior of bullying, making others suffer and offend in any way. However, more than laws and sanctions, effective and continuous education within families is needed. A restructuring in the family, building homes that function as such. A sustainable family education, free of physical and psychological violence that is the most abundant. sometimes adults don't even realize that they are abusing children is so common that it goes unnoticed, leaving large traces and wounds almost indelible. To offer children and young people the opportunity to be able to live in homes where peace and harmony are fostered and where work is done to create safe, healthy environments in search of the best welfare for them. Prevention is the most effective solution for resolving this behavior. Elaborate, create, disseminate, carry out educational campaigns through networks and all the means available. raise their voices, all united so that there are no more victims of Bullying in homes, schools; by any means, or anywhere in the world.

PSYCHOLOGICAL BULLYING

Psychological bullying is the humiliating and consistent treatment of people. It can be with or without intent, the case is that the person is a child, adolescent, or adult who ends up emotionally injured. The psychological bullying is one of the most harmful, and devastating is responsible for destroying, weakening the personality of the individual gradually diminishing its character. lowering his self-esteem. The perpetrator does not look beyond, never measures the magnitude of the suffering and the injuries that he is causing to the victim, nor the great damages that his action left behind, he does not stop to think for a single second about the consequences. Whoever does Bullying does not have time to imagine that something is happening to him, nor that he is doing a displacement, projects through Bullying that internal or external problem that affects or displeases him. Mostly those who receive the most attack are the youngsters between twelve and seventeen years of age, it is precisely they who are most affected emotionally. More than any other group because of their vulnerability, in this difficult stage of their lives, it does not mean that children and adults do not have an effect on them. For children, it is easier to get into a difficult situation if they receive good treatment in time. Otherwise they will continue with that pain until they reach adulthood, and adults as they have almost always matured their character can deal better with this type of problem, or any other presented to them, yet bullying causes suffering to the victim regardless of their age. But the ones who suffer the most are teenagers, even the simplest things are complicated. A grain of sand seems like a mountain to them, with a glance they feel their world crumbling. Bullying is always the same, in any of its forms, it's still bullying, either way the person gets hurt.

The difference is only in the form, places and means used to intimidate others and the people who do so, since over the years many perpetrators and more victims have been victims.

Children and adolescents, although it may seem strange, many adults have been victims of Bullying, the same can be done by different means and in different places. The first to start bullying children are some relatives, who do not believe that they are abusing children. This becomes a chain that reaches the schools and often extends beyond to other places. When you are satisfied there is no need to waste time to bully anyone. In the case of children, things are very different, because those who bully other children or adolescents are often just trying to get the attention of their parents, guardians, teachers or perhaps they have been victims of bullying. The children who do the bullying are presenting their voice-of-alert. Something is happening to them inside, someone might say and think that we pay a lot of attention to the perpetrator. The problem isn't with the victim, who really has a problem is the bullying individual. In short, it's the one who needs the most help, if you pay attention to whoever is attacking. There will be no more victims, the root will be eradicated once and for all. the victim is destroyed, but the wounds and lacerations that may be present inside the perpetrator are not visible to the naked eye. The perpetrator must be given attention. You need to investigate why your behavior and starting from your problem requires to be treated by a psychologist, a licensed professional. If the foundations were created for them to be emotionally satisfied at ease in his daily life, the lack of attention and affection caused negative effects on children and adolescents. But it cannot be said that there is only one cause for someone to Bully, they are multifactorial. There is no specific determining cause. We will have to look for all the elements, indicators, and possible variables that cause this misconduct. A strong family education based on values, clear rules in the home could contribute. And of course, the children are kept busy in some educational task. Since leisure has never been a good advisor, certain educational tools will help offenders in schools and homes alike. Offer them treatments to eliminate any source of aggression or violence that they carry within. Once the perpetrator's behavior has been changed, the aggression will decrease. Always taking into account all the information to which some are exposed inside and outside their family environment. If the foundations are created for them to be happy.

We will no longer have children and adolescents being victims of Bullying. The aggressors would feel complete and satisfied. They wouldn't feel the need to bother someone to solve that problem. Occupation in some activity would help them channel their anxiety by investing their time in productive things without hurting others. Busy minds offer greater results than if they are idle. However, it cannot be overlooked that children need free time to feel good about themselves, and their space to play and share with other children should always be respected. The intimidation of other children has been in the light of day, it is not new. There has always been Bullying at school and as mentioned above in most cases the root of the problem is not in the child who assaults. There is a situation that should be investigated in search of solutions. That boy, girl or adolescent, perhaps wants affection, children and adolescents have different ways of expressing their discontent with their environment. They act in some way with society, or demand attention. When they don't get it in appropriate ways, they turn to other media that often don't even realize the damage they are doing. The problem is to channel your difficulty through any channel. A kind of valve that needs to let the air escape somewhere. Psychological bullying is not only done by children and adolescents, many adults also do bullying. Some husbands, wives also do bullying to their partner or partner, sometimes begins in the courtship with small words that seem a little innocent. So much so that they may go unnoticed by the other person, but then take strength and become abuse and even domestic violence. This psychological abuse is further complicated by the fact that most of them do it in front of their children. They are learning this inappropriate behavior, they may take it to school and if left untreated, there are thousands of chances that they will pursue it all their lives by doing the same to their respective partners. A chain, a vicious circle that in some circumstances gets out of control. Psychological abuse takes hold of many homes in such a way that in some cases they end up in separation, divorce or regrettable tragedies.

There are adults who bully minors, even in their own homes they receive psychological bullying from relatives who do not measure the consequences. They do not think they are causing harm to children and/or adolescents.

Detecting bullying early before the situation gets complicated would be a very good option. The earlier we control the outbreaks of violence, the greater the results. Once the teacher detects the first signs that a child is verbally assaulting his or her partner (s). Or with simple gestures, you should try to put a stop to it, you are still on time. When the situation begins, we must try to prevent it from spreading to the entire classroom or school. You should communicate with school administrators, psychologists, and school staff who are responsible for your child's welfare. These parents should, in turn, communicate with both parents separately. If it is possible to bring them together to reach agreements that lead to the solution of the problem. And with great care, because sometimes children only reflect in school the behavior of some problem at home. When it comes to violent parents who don't recognize that their child may have a problem, the situation may become more difficult.

Far from finding solutions, other conflicts and much more serious inconveniences could arise. When they are cooperating parents, it is easy to change the inappropriate behavior of children. The reason for this is that they are parents who, although they may not have realized that their children are going through a bad time of loneliness, some have many occupations. Everyone has to work, and when they get home they can't ask their children how school has gone. Either because they are too exhausted from the daily life, or they are already asleep. A lot of parents can't see their children. Many children and teenagers who arrive from school and their parents are not at home, occupations, distance prevents it. However, a call is convenient, in this case is very important to give you that support they need. If it is not possible to be at home, there are different ways to accompany them in their daily life and in their tasks. Another situation is that some children are afraid to talk about what is happening to their parents. Sometimes intimidation goes further and some of the victims receive threats from the perpetrators. That if they talk to someone, worse could happen to them, in this case the victims do not dare to communicate with their parents. It is necessary to maintain good communication with the children so that they lose the fear of being assaulted and tell their elders about whatever they are going through. The best preventive medicine in the case of bullying in schools, both for the victim and the offender, would be that both parents and guardians are alert in everything concerning their children. Most do, no doubt, but exceptions exist. Other parents, many times, are aware of everything that happens with their children. But that's not what children feel, some demand and require far more attention than their parents can provide. Day-to-day occupations complicate the lives of adults. Situations that cannot be controlled, the problem is that as many children as adolescents need to be supervised, talked to and observed. Give them answers to their concerns and questions, without going to extremes. They will be answered according to their age, based on their questions, without lies or deceit. If you don't tell them the truth, they will look for the answers themselves through other means. Young people and children should feel loved, protected, accepted by their closest relatives. They know who loves them and tells them the truth. Their self-esteem needs to be strengthened in their minds for when someone wants to offend or hurt them, the wounds are less profound, the chances of being affected are minimal. They cannot be taken out of the outside world, rather it is to indicate to them how one can be in it, without being affected by all the good and bad things that in one way or another it may be impossible to avoid. But that some of the situations only serve to prepare them to live in a world where everything exists. We're not putting them in a crystal ball. Daily living has many demands that they will have to face. Even so, measures must be taken to prevent, stop and end bullying, let's work with children and young people to strengthen their self-esteem at home and in school. In case you can't avoid bullying; let their mind be sufficiently stable and strong enough to allow them to get out of the problem less emotionally hurt. Recalling that psychological bullying is far more destructive than any disastrous disease. Leaves wounds and scars perhaps incurable and indelible. If these don't heal, they stay there for life. We need to make a human chain. Raise your voice against school bullying, raising awareness of how dangerous it is. It is necessary to develop educational campaigns, look for all the existing tools, find solutions aimed at preventing psychological bullying before it spreads. Home, school and society, with the best existing tool, which is capable of breaking down all barriers, education.

Let us all work together for the well-being, safety, physical and mental health of children and adolescents.

BULLYING TO TRANSGENDER PEOPLE AND/OR OTHER PREFERENCES

The term transgender refers to someone who has a certain birth sex, but identifies with the opposite, either female or male.

It may be that a boy or girl from an early age may not feel comfortable with the sex that has come. They feel trapped in a body that is not their own. This has nothing to do with who their parents are or what society the child or the family belongs to. They can occur anywhere in the world, even if their parents have obtained a birth certificate with the name of a female or male, this person feels that it is not he or she to whom the parents recognize. Inside her interior if she is a girl, she identifies herself with a boy and when she is a boy, she feels she is a girl. This situation could become a problem for him or her depending on how his or her parents assimilate and handle the situation. For some parents, it may be a great difficulty. Meanwhile, for other parents, there would be no problem in accepting the sex that their son or daughter prefers, or rather the one they identify with and feel comfortable with. It is complicated when the girl feels male or the boy feels female and the parents do not understand how this can happen to them. Some people tend to feel confused, disappointed, frustrated, and a little disappointed, there are those who do not accept this situation under any pretext. They end up despising and marginalizing the son or daughter. While some more understanding ones don't make much of a difference if your child prefers one sex or another. For them the most important thing is their child and their happiness, and the rest is secondary, but these are some exceptions. Some don't care what other people, relatives, friends and neighbors will say. While other parents pay a lot of attention to the opinions of others without thinking about the best welfare for their son or daughter. They prefer a sad and depressed son or daughter over accepting him or her and letting him or her live the way he or she wants and prefers. The fact is that some more conservative parents are afraid of bullying that they, as well as their sons and daughters, will suffer. Because in various societies they do not accept transgender people, or with another orientation or preference. Not everyone is prepared to accept that someone mocks or teases his or her relative, much less when it comes to his or her child. The next drawback is when children have to attend school, who are victims of bullying by other children and/or adolescents. This situation creates a major problem for them, there is no reason why someone should be a victim of bullying, even if the person is an adult. But when you are a boy or girl, especially for teenagers it is harder to deal with bullying. Many times, the situation in this case becomes very difficult to resolve, for a simple reason, if the children who are going through this conflict do not feel understood and supported by their parents and relatives. When they arrive at the schools that the other children and / or adolescents Bullying them, not being able to express themselves openly could generate a state of anxiety, despair, sadness, stress, insomnia, anorexia, bulimia, anxiety, depression, and a series of psychological indolent problems; If left unattended in time, they could become a more complicated problem, and go to extremes that could get out of hand for both parents and the school system. For this reason, it is important for the teacher to be alert. Once the minimum rate of bullying is detected, corrections must be made in time so that the problem does not spread to major complications, which are more serious and difficult to correct. The school officials should be notified at the minimum outbreak of violence by one adolescent child or another, and the parents should be contacted immediately to find solutions together. To solve the problem before it gets complicated by escaping everyone's control.

For the same boy or girl who feels trapped in another person's body, it is already a problem, even if it is a small one, because all children must attend school, finding in it safety; a place not only welcoming, but safe, where they can have an active participation in class without fear of being bothered by others. At the same time, parents feel safe so that they can carry out their activities without any worries that someone might attack their children. When children are on campus, it is the responsibility of the school to keep students safe. Of course, from time to time some variables become uncontrollable, however, the school is responsible for all children within it.

Some adults also suffer because they cannot manifest themselves as they want to be, they are afraid of facing a society that often discriminates against them, marginalizes them.

It does not allow them to identify themselves as they are. They bully them, attack them, not only psychologically; they have seen some extremes where they have been physically assaulted by the mere fact of wanting to feel comfortable with the person with whom they identify. The rights of every human being are inalienable. No motive will be valid for anyone to be offended or assaulted, for their preference in a world where technology and science have been growing at gigantic levels. People should have the freedom to be able to be as they want, without fear of being rejected, let alone victimized by bullying. As long as their behavior does not affect others or the society in which they operate, people have the right to enjoy freedom of movement like all citizens who have not violated the laws of society. Some boys who show a level of education or fine manners tend to receive Bullying.

YES, it is a girl with certain mannerisms that the person understands are typical of boys who receive Bullying. That must not continue. When a man has good manners, and some women are also victims of bullying if they show behavior that for some people is typical of men or vice versa. Even in the midst of a world with so much progress, where society has reached levels that have crossed all borders; a totally globalized world, people are victims of bullying. As the world is constantly evolving, it is necessary to put in place the necessary tools to prevent and eradicate Bullying. No one should have to suffer or be intimidated by anything but their sexual preference.

Bullying is violence in disguise. A monster, which must be paid attention to for the good of society. This problem must not continue.

Educating for peace must be the purpose of all to offer a better society to the youngest and youngest.

The only thing that generates violence is more violence and destruction, today is a very important moment to think about joining forces to make Bullying disappear; there are no more people distressed and saddened by Bullying. It is everyone's right to feel safe. Safe like others free to live in a society where people do not feel vulnerable. Don't be afraid to go out somewhere or just walk freely through the streets without fear of being bullied, as long as that freedom doesn't cause harm to other living beings.

The best place in the world to live is a place where peace reigns and people's rights are respected. Without affecting ours.

Treat everyone with the respect they deserve for being a person, regardless of who they are or want to be, the autonomy and independence of others must be respected.

Not everyone has the facility to face the world around them, regardless of criticism and opinions. Sometimes the closest relatives are the first ones to start tags from childhood, and for this reason as they have already been assaulted. They may feel fragile, sensitive to face the world outside. Or some people who find it difficult to accept and respect the rights of others. It seems very easy for someone to deal with this problem, but not all people have the same courage to come out in the midst of the storm. Only a few are brave enough to shout to the four winds for what they are. They feel and want to be without paying attention to criticism and bullying. There are those who find it difficult to succeed, and end up immersing themselves in anxiety, depression. They go through life frightened, saddened and unable to get up. Without forgetting those who feel shy, withdrawn, and ashamed, and others less fortunate go to extremes, causing harm to themselves, because they do not endure that terrible nightmare. Bullying has a very high cost. Lives that are being lost because of you. It's time to look for possible solutions just as it is done with a number of diseases, not that this is a disease. Rather, it is a social problem that affects everyone, without exception. Society groans in pain when someone makes a drastic decision to be a victim of Bullying.

All people without exception deserve to live in a just society that gives everyone the rights they deserve as human beings. Let each one of us manifest however we want to, without being subjected to aggression.

The problem is that those who do the bullying never think it is aggression or violence. Of course, bullying is violence, only disguised. Above all, it has not been given the attention it requires.

It is important to educate our children to respect the rights of others and to be convinced that they too deserve respect.

BULLYING AMONG WOMEN

Someone might ask, what is it? What does Bullying among women mean? Oh, bullying among women does exist. Even if it is not identified as such, the problem is that it is a bullying left unnoticed, let alone identified. But there is a lot of verbal and psychological violence between women. They receive Bullying for their body, their way of dressing, and for a series of things without importance, a kind of fight without quarter. Many times, bullying is personal, by phone or social networks is where it is exposed. Any problems, no matter if the person is going through grief. Pain or anguish, adding discomfort to your distress, at your fingertips.

Whose only intention is to cause suffering. A kind of bitter taste, because the laws of the universe charge and pay everyone in the same way. How many times have you heard one or more women insult even those who think they are friends? They laugh at their situation, whatever it is. There are cases where women receive bullying and murmurings both in public and private. Just because it's not at the latest fashion, because they don't belong to the same society or race, or their car is not new. Because they are thin, or the opposite. They bully someone else for not wearing makeup. The name given to a woman who doesn't wear makeup is the "simple one". Violating the rights of everyone as a person to wear makeup or not, without having to receive bullying for it. Girls and boys watch and listen as some adults bully their friends.

A real friend of mine would never bully the other one. On the contrary, when they see that something is not going well, that it is detrimental to them, they would let them know in good form without hurting their esteem or feelings. With respect so your friend won't be offended.

Some women do Bullying to others, just because they have different purchasing power. Without thinking that having a state; economic solvency can be temporary. Life is full of ups and downs. Even the mountains and large trees tend to collapse, and the small trees have time to grow. Life is full of surprises. Solidarity magnifies us, elevating us to the top of the summit. Criticism, if not, diminishes us, it serves as a cover letter.

We have learned of people who have had abundance on all levels, empires. Power, in every sense of the word, but from one day to the next they have fallen into mismanagement and / or because they have been left in the hands of dishonest people, have lost it all. It is not right for someone to be bullying because of their economic position, or anything existing in society.

Today we have, tomorrow we don't know. Someone who doesn't have one today to buy a bottle of water the next day could buy the whole spring. We have seen and had the unpleasant disgrace of hearing some women speak disparagingly of others; hurting them without mercy. Others less direct use social networks, the telephone to try to attack one than other women.

If women were more supportive of each other. Perhaps it would serve to lower the levels of violence against women.

Women deserve respect. No one should be abused or offended. It is women who are the most delicate beings that nature has created. They possess the delicacy and freshness of roses, but at the same time are strong. That power of resistance, struggle, and self-improvement that they have is incomparable.

Women are tireless, it's not right for them to be disregarded. If women did not exist, the world would become extinct. They are the ones who by divine order were given the privilege of bringing human beings into their wombs, to support them for nine long months. Almost always, taking care of them, educating them, and in many occasions supporting them, there are many who have had to take care of their children themselves. Support them, because for one reason or another, they have been left alone with all the responsibilities of the household. Women warriors who have fought with great determination. They have fought against wind and tide, without letting the adversities of life consume them. Greater results would be obtained if instead of bullying, all women join regardless of religion, race, color, nationality, economic status, or any situation that some are going through to prevent, diminish, end bullying. And end to all forms of violence against women. Altogether, to create a better society where peace, harmony, respect and respect reign, where they and children can live in violence-free homes.

Letting everyone live their own way, as long as they don't harm someone with their behavior, in the best way they can and want. Without being subjected to censorship or having to feel trapped in a world that demands of them; to be beautiful, they must be thin, slender, with an extremely flat belly, extremely thin waist, firm bust, and a series of stereotypical things that do not correspond to reality.

If a woman doesn't meet these standards, she's no longer pretty. The worst thing is that it is women themselves who maintain this competition between them.

Every woman is beautiful and interesting, to be beautiful all she needs is to be a woman, regardless of her physical attractiveness, age or condition, she should not be a victim of Bullying.

Psychological bullying turns women into victims, there must be some way to stop it. Because women should be treated with respect and distinction. For their great role in being women, and for all the functions they perform. Not only do they care for families, they are the other half of the world, they contribute to the development of the nation with enthusiasm, they are tireless, the different tasks they have to perform in any regulation are carried out with care and devotion. If you are looking for a being of inexhaustible strength, do not go far, in a woman you will find it. She plays all the roles that life has given her with love, dedication. Women are full of courage and strength at the same time. Women in one way or another offer a large share of their country's development. Because she is a woman and for all her cooperation, her contribution, her sweetness, delicacy, tenderness and love for her family deserves only distinction and respect. She's a source of love, she must receive that very thing, love. Let us hope that solidarity reigns, together, a little bit of conscience and instead of violence, verbal, psychological, physical or by any other means, that it contributes to peace in the world, and that no woman feels offended. That their esteem does not go down simply because they do not look, or do not have the stereotypes of recent times. A woman, regardless of race, society, creed, color or level of purchase, should feel free to be who she wants to be, to play the role she wants to choose, without feeling devalued. Let no one offend her or belittle her esteem for any reason, that every woman may express herself freely and live in a home, and in a world where she feels valued. Never to be discriminated against for being a woman. Being a woman is priceless is invaluable, a woman is and will always be more valuable than all the precious garments put together. For a number of qualities, it possesses, she must be respected, loved, distinguished with the highest distinctions. She deserves to be exalted and awarded with the highest laurels. Bullying among women whose mantle has different colors, without being perceived as Bullying must reach its final point.

The less violence there is among women, the more there will be no room or space for a single woman to feel offended, assaulted, or abused. Let us all fight together as a society so that no woman in the world will receive any kind of violence. Let's start at home by teaching children and adolescents that both females and males should respect and be respected. Competition between women could become violence. In the same way, boys should be educated about the value of women and their great value in society and all the roles that they and no one else has to play, and they do so with humility. Without thinking about the great effort, I have to make, a woman is always willing. She does not look at obstacles, barriers or frontiers, she does all the work with determination, love and great tenacity. It is necessary to educate children and adolescents about the value of the person in order to reduce levels of violence. Let everyone recognize the value of women without minimizing men, let there be respect between the parties and let there be healthy and diplomatic dialogue for the resolution of conflicts between all human beings.

Both deserve respect. It is domestic work, so that when children become adults, they can treat women with dignity, and vice versa, but it is work that must be done from childhood. Girls must be taught not to criticize others. Regardless of their condition. Bullying among women must disappear so that there is not a single indicator that promotes violence against women.

BULLYING AT WORK

The place where a person works, many times becomes like a second home, is where they stay most of the time, depending on the tasks, jobs, or functions that each person performs, and for which they have been trained; trained individually, physically, psychologically, mentally, technically empirically and/or intellectually.

Very few people work inside their homes. Others have their own business, and maybe things will be made easier for them to have a business. But to maintain a company brings with it many responsibilities and commitments that not all people are willing to take on. The fact is that, in one way or another, almost all of us are under the obligation to do some work in order to subsist and live in a dignified manner in a globalized and competitive consumer society. Regardless of the people, or nation where we live. Knowing that a job allows people to feel safe and contributes to development and a better quality of life. From generation to generation people have done some trade, of the kind that this or their preference.

To support your family and your own person, not all the activities you do can be done in your own home and much less alone.

It will always require the labor of other people, as well as a certain ability to perform some tasks that it is necessary to use the intellect of a trained and trained staff. Because otherwise that business, whatever it is, wouldn't work. Even if there is an owner, manager, contractor, or representative, the collaboration of different types of competent personnel is of paramount importance for any corporation, however small, to achieve the desired and expected goals of those who have created it. It is likely that in the not too distant future robots will perform some functions and perform certain trades and tasks. There will come a time when those in charge of battle are not the humans. Robots will perform a large part of the activities; the machines and the big ships will be piloted by robots. They will build the big buildings, the towers; and a series of tasks that will be done by robots. A large part of the manpower that men and women make today will be replaced by robots, human losses will be less and many of the functions of the present. In the not too distant future it will be robots who will carry out these tasks, they will be the ones who will take care of and clean people's houses. They will remove snow, cut grass and trees, plant and gather fruit to feed people. Even much of people's food will be made and prepared by humanoid robots. Even the big factories will turn to robots for different tasks, they will build big buildings, bridges, and roads, we will have some master robots. They will clean the windows of the huge skyscrapers so there will be no need for someone to risk their lives and fall down. They will not only do most of the activities, but they will be able to interact and perform specific functions, receive all kinds of commands. Technological breakthroughs will reach breakthrough levels. The future that awaits us in terms of technology is quite promising and exceptional. However, the human hand can never be totally displaced, there will always be jobs where the hand will be needed. The capacity and above all, the human intellect; although labor can be replaced and certain activities. However, the power possessed by the human mind is unique and irreplaceable. This capacity of human thinking is fundamental and irreplaceable. There is a very simple word, as well as others that must be taken into account and put into practice for any corporation to achieve the desired goals. That's: HARMONY. Harmony between all the people who have the opportunity to form a team to perform the different functions that need to be performed in a company, large or small. The drawback is that sometimes the smaller it gets, the less harmony there is, although everyone has their own tasks and work to do. Some are overwhelmed by a great deal of dissatisfaction, leading them to create a certain degree of conflict in a subtle way. Starting with simple words that at first seem innocent. But deep down they are intended to cause annoyance and restlessness, gestures, looks, among other things, that attack their companions. At first, they may go unnoticed even by the recipient. But, not satisfied whoever does it is raising the tone and what is worse, extending it to other comrades, some end up in solidarity with the one who does the bullying, they see it as something normal, others with the victim. God has given me the opportunity to work.

In different places and with different people of different ages, with varied occupations, professions and tasks different from those of others. Noting the dissatisfaction of a few, even though they are exercising their profession for which they have been prepared. However, with a certain discontent, being demonstrated, when they begin to do Bullying to one or another of their co-workers. Without thinking that everyone's work is important. Let's imagine that they were all doctors, lawyers, who would teach children, adolescents and other adults who still want to learn and thereby a number of activities that are necessary. In diversity, that is where the beauty of life lies, it is satisfying and beautiful that each individual can achieve his or her dreams and carry out the tasks, tasks and trades they like best; for which he or she has been trained or is within their reach.

If everyone performed the same functions, the others would be left adrift without finding someone else to do them. The world needs and always will need people who can carry out different activities, because that is precisely what makes people develop. If we look at a large tree, it is true that we can only look at it from the trunk to the branches, but it would not be a tree without the roots. It doesn't mean that they have less value because they are underneath. The trunk, which extends up to the top, the branches, leaves, flowers, fruits, a company is similar to a tree where each of the tasks that each person performs is of paramount importance; and like all the parts that form the tree whatever it is.

Although the roots are beneath the ground, someone is likely to think they are less important than the trunk, or the leaves could scream at the four winds that they are more. Because they are very high but each of the parts form the whole. Together they are the ones that make the tree what it is, a great tree, equally in a company, public or private, both the trades and those who carry them out will always be essential, so that it works and reaches the goal. Achieving the objectives dreamt of by those who created it. However, so that it has a great scope and development. A good harmony is essential for it to function as such. Any focus of Bullying, a small drop of dissatisfaction from those who work in it. It is detrimental to both the staff and the development of the corporation.

It is not always the case that some employees Bullying their peers, because the majority of institutions have very clear, defined and well-established rules. They do not allow staff working on it to have any conflict, immediately, to observe something out of place. Take appropriate measures and corrective measures. The place where people work is sacred, as much as the home should be. Peace, harmony, companionship, solidarity and above all respect must reign. When you take on the commitment to perform a task or trade function, a job is an agreement between both parties. Not only with the company and its executives, but also with itself and the function that everyone must perform, it must be done with enthusiasm, dedication, motivation and care.

That the goal besides earning a living. Where they offer us the opportunity to grow one way or another; Be a Bullying free place. This evil causes pain and sadness, discouragement, no matter where on the planet people are, it leads nowhere. It produces stress, anxiety, grief, and pain, secondly whoever does the bullying will end up outside the company. Whatever function you perform, it requires enthusiasm, motivation, giving your best and allowing others to do the same.

People's role requires a certain degree of tranquility and concentration because any distraction would not only reduce work or production, but sometimes even an accident could occur. This type of bullying is not only harmful to the company. It is also available to all its members, regardless of their role.

Although this type of bullying may be subtle, it is also detrimental to the victim.

It produces great anxiety, anguish, stress, and even despair. Reaching the point of wanting to leave their place of employment. But the very need for economic development forces him to remain in it, even though he feels intimidated. Although sometimes things get out of control, so that those who are victims of Bullying have to escape to end this problem. And, what is worse, on several occasions it transcends beyond the place where people work. Bullying or bullying is harmful to victims, because it deteriorates the emotional tranquility that all people have a right to feel. In any space or place where they are located, especially when it is one of the most sacred places for any person. Where one earns his daily bread, should be as sacred as the home, free from harassment. Bullying whatever and wherever it occurs must be prevented, stopped, controlled and eliminated for the good and mental health of individuals and society.

POSSIBLE CAUSES OF BULLYING AT SCHOOL

The causes are multi-factorial, different are the causes; diverse and disastrous are the consequences of bullying in schools. It has reached such high levels that in recent times it has gone from school to a social problem.

It is very likely that Bullying originated in a remote time.

No exact date is recorded that states this is when Bullying began. Nor is it a specific place from which it originated, but there have always been victims and perpetrators, both in schools and homes. As in various workplaces, and countless public and private places, where children, adolescents and adults in one way or another have been intimidated and mocked. It is not a new practice that has emerged today. However, there was Bullying by phone, only before cyber Bullying, if it existed was timid, moderate, subtle. Social networks had not achieved that preponderant place that they now boast. They have been a great push on all the economic and social fronts, a great platform, a good advance, all over the world for the union and development of peoples, in general with them we can guarantee that we have made giant strides forward, in society. Without a doubt, they are one of the biggest links. They have served to save lives, bring families together, meet people, keep us informed of what is happening in faraway lands and a host of benefits they offer. However, some individuals use them inadequately.

The world has become globalized through technology and social networks. In addition to a series of inventions that other people have bequeathed for the benefit of all humanity. It is very difficult to label and specify a possible sustainable cause, which can be identified as the only one that leads a perpetrator to annoy and intimidate the victim.

In reality, the causes are as diverse as the places, the victims and the perpetrators, each human being has a different history that he has had to live in his long or short life. A person's experiences are very different from those of others, even if they come from the same household and family. Sometimes, even though they are twin brothers, their experiences and stories differ from each other, each person is unique. As a unique and individual entity, it faces the setbacks that life brings in a very different way to others. Twin brothers and/or twins and / or twins if for no reason to their will grow apart, there will be much more difference in the way they behave and face the challenges of life. There are so many situations that cause someone to cause discomfort to their victim. Everyone will have a different motivation. One might think that those who perform this action have no motive, that they do it without realizing it and without thinking that this is a problem and that they do not intend to hurt, lacerate, emotionally destroy or take a person to extremes. Those who engage in this practice at first glance may not realize why they are doing it, nor the extent or number of problems. And hardships that he would give up his action even when they know what they're doing. They never have any idea of the problem that comes with bullying someone. If the perpetrators are teenagers at that age, there are no consequences. Not even in the pain or physical or psychological wounds that they caused not only to one person, to many. The families are directly or indirectly involved, including the victimizer's families who will have to assume responsibility in some way. Of course, the victims' families are the most affected when one of their members is attacked or intimidated by Bullying. If a child or teenager does not want to attend school, they become depressed, cry, sleep a lot, and change their behavior.

Because someone else is bothering you, both family and school as a rule have to get involved. The school cannot isolate itself from the family or relatives of the school; there must be a good relationship between the two. They should work together as a team, for the benefit and well-being of students.

It is true that in some situations it appears that there are no apparent reasons. But it will always have some latent root, even if you can't see at first glance that it causes someone to bother someone else is small, or adult, in a verbal or psychological way, it can be the case that the problem that drives a child or adolescent to bully his or her partner. It has nothing to do with the school, nor with the victim, the perpetrator could be making a displacement. Because of any problems in the family environment, domestic violence often becomes a trigger for children to tease others. The lack of peace and harmony in some homes creates insecurity, anxiety and anguish in children and young people, causing them to bring this violence to school against their peers, the loneliness of daily life. There are many who spend long hours at home alone, because their parents must work to support them. Emotional abuse, physical and psychological violence, economic inequality, lack of values, clear rules in the home, dysfunctional homes, domestic violence. Prohibited substance use, alcoholism, physical and verbal abuse of children, neglect, neglect, inattention, and lack of affection. Extreme poverty could become a trigger for violence; lack of communication, children and adolescents have many concerns and questions that need to be answered. There are countless causes that could be provoking inappropriate behavior of children and/or adolescents in the classroom and/or school. Sometimes it becomes impossible to detect what happens inside a child's mind or interior to attack others and spread the aggression. Other children may be more likely to participate. When it comes to adolescents, they tend to be supportive of their group. To such a high degree that they take other people's causes as their own in order to be on the side of their classmates, and on several occasions, they involve boys who have nothing to do with school. They only come together because one of them knows the perpetrator. This happens when they go to extremes. It is no longer the simple Bullying of words, psychological intimidation rises to another level they go to physical aggressions, pushes and blows. The problem is that it's always the victim who gets hurt the most.

One group joins together to cause physical harm to another child or adolescent.

I had the bitterness and unhappiness of having to witness several incidents in the different schools where I worked for several years. In high school, the levels of violence and aggression are higher. It was neither easy nor flattering to watch some teenagers convene a group to attack others. Perhaps for nothing for a simple glance, because someone who arrived earlier kept a chair for his friend. Perhaps because the young man did not like someone else, for a girl, a boy, a chair, on one occasion a girl hit a young man with a chair, causing them a great wound on his face. This was all about the chair, apparently. But deep down, the girl had other problems in the family that were beyond her control. Very strong for his little teenage brain of thirteen. An abusive, ruthless, arrogant, abusive father beat her and took all the money she worked for, to go betting on horses and all kinds of games she had at her fingertips. If the daughter tried to intervene, she would beat her too.

The young woman could do nothing to defend her mother, because he was her father. The difficulty was that the problem went outside, that incident didn't stay there. The next day the police came looking for the student and immediately the injured person's parents searched for a lawyer. The entire school and teaching staff were involved. In this problem, which spread outside of it, it was necessary to work with both families to reach an agreement so that things did not get worse. This was not the only case, however, with many verbal, physical and psychological assaults at school. In which the entire educational community had the obligation and duty to intervene, both with one family and the other. A student problem cannot be solved without the collaboration and participation and consent of families. Under no circumstances, however much the school wants, the most important parts are the relatives of the young people. Without their presence, there will be no possible solutions. Once it was the case that a high school freshman of fourteen years old, exchanged a few words on the court with a seventeen-year-old, from the same high school. Everyone left the court and went to their classrooms, but nobody had the slightest idea how the youngest one called a group of young people who had nothing to do with school, brought clubs and things no one could imagine. Of course, they did not carry firearms, but yes, others that need not be mentioned, and even a large dog to attack the last year student. They waited for them outside the school and were beaten together, they only left him alive, but unrecognizable. The biggest one went to a hospital. For several months, as expected, other classmates who had already been mistreated entered the fight, when teachers realized what was happening outside the school. The young man was already lying on the injured pavement everywhere, unable to return to school for a long time. He almost lost his life and the last year of school, the aggressor was fired from the campus. Something that began with simple words reached those extremes. Aggressions among young people start with words, shove and end in blows and sometimes go further.

These are events that didn't just happen in high school. In other schools the same thing has happened and happens, that a student has a problem with one and so many others are involved that have nothing to do with that campus. I hope that solutions can be found to this situation, which does not only belong in schools and starts in many different places. Reaching out to the most vulnerable students. This Bullying problem has ended with many young people leaving them wounded, broken, sad, physically and psychologically assaulted. As a society, it is time to look for tools to lower the levels of violence in schools. In this period called adolescence all females and males have hormonal changes. They are not very tolerant, at the slightest provocation they get upset, most teenagers do not understand tolerance. They tend to reply to a simple look. The young people of yesterday, today and tomorrow are not and will not be the exception to the rule. Many young people are neither aggressors, nor violent. But it is so much the bullying they receive from others that they go from victim to perpetrator. They end up attacking those who bullied them. On several occasions, the problem has resulted in irreparable damage, which is regrettable.

Although not everything depends on the work done by parents at home since childhood.

Some children and young people receive care and support from them, but when they get together with others they end up forgetting what they learned at home. Families do everything humanly possible to ensure that their children behave well at home, at school, and in society in general. However, they are intimidated and bullied even for being different in the sense that they maintain correct behavior in and out of school. They are often attacked for being quiet and excellent students.

When a situation of this category occurs, parents of students with good behavior may feel discouraged and helpless, since they have taken great care to educate their children at home, so that they are better individuals. When something like this happens, the solution is to address the superiors of the schools so that everyone can work in search of solutions to the Bullying situation by calling parents or guardians. Many children are not fortunate enough to live with them, which is already a big problem. the absence of one or both parents can create a vacuum of loneliness within the children, even a conflict with themselves, feeling abandoned by their parents. Other times they live with both of them, but some are very rigid or very permissive. Both situations are generators of violence, they could give rise to inappropriate and indiscipline behavior. Some parents leave their children on their own, they don't have clear parameters and rules to follow. Discipline is conspicuous by its absence, children can do and thwart everything they find in their path. Other parents correct their children with physical and verbal aggressions, instill fear, their boys fear them. A few continue with the practices of past centuries where they beat the children to discipline them, maintaining these obsolete methods. And unhealthy destroyers of character and personality that far from shaping and educating end up creating more problems for children and adolescents. This way of disciplining with violence and beatings produces only anxiety, sadness, anguish and depression for children and young people. It has a negative, devastating and irreversible effect, instead of rendering them calm, respectful, respectful, you transform them into aggressive, spiteful, distrustful, hostile and rebellious beings at the end of the day they will be adults that drag them along with all this; and many more problems.

Absent parents, it's not like they're no longer alive or traveling, are absent because they don't care at all about what they do or what happens to their children. Whether they attend school or not, they don't care; they are at home living with their children, they just feed them. I met a woman who lived with her three children and her husband. At lunchtime, she gave the children a soda and bread because for her, the television set had a higher priority than the children.

A child or young person who does not eat enough nutrients for their physical and mental development.

If you are hungry, you will not function well in your body or in your physical and emotional development. There would even be a chance that they might behave aggressively with other classmates in school. The brains of children and young people who are not properly fed will not function with the proper capacity, which they would have if they received the proteins and nutrients necessary for their normal growth and development. Some may be cared for and well fed. However, a physical health problem that is not related to the environment could cause a change in their behavior. By hurting them, not only others, themselves, children need to be taken to the doctor, a regular check-up, it is convenient to know how healthy they are.

In addition to aggressive parents, permissive, overprotective, absent, there are many children orphaned from living parents, who abandon them without noticing the harm they are doing to them; psychologically and emotionally. Some let them go around the world alone to defend themselves as they can. Other good dads leave them with relatives who in most cases abuse them, verbally, physically and all kinds of abuse.

I wish all abandoned and neglected children could find a home to take them in and treat them as they deserve because they are children.

All of us as a society, united together, can and must provide solutions. Place a grain of sand so that bullying stops, is eradicated from the home and school. Of all places, bullying affects us all as a society. Let's begin by teaching our children that all people deserve respect, tolerance, solidarity, even if their race, color, creed, and/or any other characteristics they possess are not ours. People deserve to be respected regardless of their condition, whether they are children, adolescents or adults.

They remain a unique, valuable and important human being who deserves to be treated with dignity. No matter who the person is. It is only enough to start at the first school, home, respect is a human value that must be instilled in children from an early age. Teach them to respect diversity, plants, trees, animals, all species, they are on the planet for some cause or reason and they should be taught to respect human beings. You may be anxious to know how to teach a young child these values. It is very easy for adults to lay the foundation stone, respecting the rights of that child. When adults set the example, they are like sponges, they will be absorbing, little by little until they learn to respect their elders, their companions, their little friends and themselves. If someone has no respect for their own person, it is very difficult for them to have the least respect for other living beings.

True education begins at home. This is where children have their first contact when they come out of their mother's womb. No matter how much information they receive from the outside world, all those who have learned from their parents will be a great platform for their future growth. The basis of education must start at home, especially in the first five years of life, these will be decisive in their future development. However, the education of children is a constant task; it is not a matter of a day, a week or a month, nor a year, it requires follow-up. Until adulthood, it is the responsibility of parents to bring people into society.

Migration has sown its little seed. Many parents are forced to travel to different places for unimaginable reasons, they have to leave their children in the hands of relatives, friends and neighbors. Staying with people foreign to their relatives creates nostalgia, anxiety, sadness, a great emptiness that there are no material goods that can fill. Some become spiteful rebels, violent. When children go to school, some are victims of bullying, just because they don't live with their parents, people when they go to other countries, do so in search of a better well-being for their family. And in order to offer them a better and higher quality of life. The problem is that sometimes there are things that don't work out the way you think, and you could lose more than you earned.

Some parents have the joy of being able to take them with them wherever they go, which is an idea that in principle can be good. However, if these parents travel to a country or region where the language, culture and customs differ from their own. Children will need to learn the language, and a number of other things, in that time frame, children need to be able to adapt to all these kinds of new situations for them, their peers, the system and the new teachers.

They may still be victims of bullying by other children, if they have not been taught to respect others. Children must be educated to understand that diversity exists, but they are not obliged to accept. Migrant children would only have to wait a minimum of time to quickly become familiar with the place and language spoken. Parents find it harder when they are forced to separate from their children. Such a beautiful and valuable time will never be recovered, except that the circumstances of each person's life are individual, unique, and different, and unquestionable. All people's decisions must be respected, it is not right to tell someone how or how they should act unless they ask for an opinion. Still, one must act with subtleties. It is an inalienable right of every individual to do with his life as he sees fit. The economic inequality in which many children live could become a trigger for violence, pushing them to bullying other children.

In some regions, many children are forced to go to work instead of school. are being denied the right to prepare for a better future and to integrate productively into a changing society. More and more people need to be prepared and trained.

More technicians in the bitterness of branches that exists, but children who work instead of going to school do it to make a living or to help older people with their livelihoods. It's only fair that everyone attends school. No child or adolescent should stop studying. There are no valid excuses for children not going to school. It is an inalienable right that must not be changed under any pretext. Children or adolescents who do not go to school become vulnerable to any situation. For this reason, they should not be robbed of their right to go to a school to prepare themselves to face a world that is subject to change and usually keeps moving. Many of the children who don't even go to school because of this are often victims of Bullying.

Most teachers do a good job of avoiding bullying in their classroom. But there's not much they can do because time is limited. They do not spend all day at school, within the school environment, they could put in place cooperative controls to foster tolerance, harmony, companionship and peace among students. But sometimes things get out of control without teachers being able to avoid confrontations. In addition, when aggressions and fights come out of school no teachers. Even if he wanted to, he can't have control. That's when they feel powerless, because certain situations are beyond their reach, both the students and the bullying students. As the victim, in most cases they do not respond academically either, it is already a double problem that originates inside and outside the classroom.

Teachers know that this issue transcends school boundaries. And no matter how much they do, it will be difficult for them to resolve this situation, unless the family cooperates. In some cases, the adult encourages aggressive behavior in minors. Far from forming peaceful children, they are formed on the basis of violent behavior, as mentioned in previous chapters, they are labeled. You're this or that, they don't realize they're being assaulted.

Causing them more harm than good. Tearing their mind, wounding their feelings, lowering their esteem, damaging their character and personality, whose damage could be permanent and irreparable. Everything that's told the kids they are today. That's what they'll become tomorrow, with rare exceptions. The lack of a family education based on values: Respect, companionship, understanding, affection, responsibility, tolerance, solidarity. The absence of a parent in the home in some cases can lead children to become victims or perpetrators, the constant arguments and quarrels between them, when the mother and father do not agree to educate the children. One wants to implement a very rigid discipline and perhaps the other one is quite flexible. Others tend to give the child every taste but are opposed by the other parent. In short, the child does not know what to abstain from. Households living in constant disagreement regarding the education of their children. Children who grow up in totally dysfunctional homes, where there is no parent to protect them, are much more vulnerable to any type of attack, including bullying. Any type of domestic violence, domestic violence, skewing the balance more towards one child than the other when there is more than one. Parents who spoil one child and not the other. Showing them more affection, or having preferred children, all of these innocent and unconscious parental behaviors generate behavioral changes in children and young people.

Some withdraw by becoming submissive and shy and others violent and aggressive with their classmates in school or the classroom. Other times with his own brothers. Another situation that affects boys by changing their behavior is the error that some parents who have two or more children make comparison between one and the other. In addition to the children of choice are the marginalized. Those that no one pays attention to, or perhaps it is those that children perceive. It may be the case that in practice parents do not make any exceptions other than the boys' feelings. Everyone should be treated the same way, everyone is favored. This leads to problems in children and even enmity between siblings.

Divorce from both parents creates insecurity when they are not handled properly. When the separation is not only between couples, it includes children. The fact that one parent puts the child against the other parent, telling them it is bad, creates sadness and insecurity in them. Some parents are not divorced, but one parent tends to talk horrors about the other parent in front of the children. All of these, in short, without adults noticing it, end up affecting the behavior of minors. Parents' addiction to prohibited substances is detrimental to their children's behavior.

Socioeconomic inequality, seeing that some children and/or adolescents enjoy things and certain privileges that they would like to have and cannot, because their parents do not have the power to do so at this moment. It could create a feeling of bitterness and inferiority. They must be taught that no child studying is poor. Even if they lack some material things today, studying can be achieved. With efforts, we achieve all the things that are in the world, we just have to wait a little. When parents are loving and affectionate with their children, they take less account of financial needs. Encourage them to always study even if their parents have not been able to achieve higher education.

It is necessary to give the attention and dedication that young people and children require. Building tolerant homes full of affection, understanding, and a great deal of patience is not an easy task; raising children to be good men and women demands love and a series of values that must be included in the education of future adults.

Starting in the homes to cut off all the possible variables and causes that lead to bullying. Contributing to the fact that it is born and grows like weeds in the middle of a beautiful rose garden, home schooling, first school.

It is a way of preventing, preventing it from being born and spreading to educational centers, at the same time it will become extinct elsewhere. If anyone thinks it's something impossible that's beyond our reach. Certainly not, because not everyone does bullying. Not all young people are victims or perpetrators. It means that if you can work at home to get those who do Bullying to behave in accordance with the norms and standards of society.

Not everyone is violent and aggressive. Parents take care of working with their children and for their children, they dedicate time to them, otherwise they can offer quality.

Even if they don't have enough time to devote to them for the sake of careers.

They talk to them. They offer them security, not only financial security, their children recognize that their parents are the ones who have adopted or conceived them. They live for them, and because of them. Parents who make every effort and do everything in their power to ensure that their children are good people. You can live for your children without parents neglecting their other responsibilities as adults, and without neglecting their personal lives. Most people make them, work and meet all the standards, without neglecting their commitments as parents. Nothing is impossible. If we all work together to reduce the causes, there will be no bullying. There will be no more victims or perpetrators. The work does not consist of going against the perpetrator is, to form children and young people to live in society. It is much broader work, prevention and education always serve as platforms for behavior change in an individual. Educate the child today, it's the only way not to have to punish the adult tomorrow.

THE CONSEQUENCES OF BULLYING

The consequences are as diverse as the causes, the problems arising from a Bullying attack are many.

The pain and suffering and a whole rainbow of problems that leaves the victim after bullying. It is not possible to mention them; the list wouldn't be long enough. Space would be the space to present all the negative effects of this serious problem.

A set of complications derived from bullying, to which we should attach vital importance. A child who has been a victim of bullying, isolates himself, doesn't socialize with others, loses all interest in having little friends because of fear, insecurity, anxiety. He fears being assaulted, at school he avoids all contact with the other children and does not want to go out on the field. He doesn't participate in sports anymore. When there is a celebration at school they don't share. Refuse to be present at activities. Most suffer from low esteem, feel ugly, inferior to others, believe that they are useless, that they are not smart like the other children in their classroom, their school, and their environment. Children who used to be happy become sad. If she liked school, they end up losing all motivation and don't want to go or run away. They lower their grades, bright students with excellent results, we can see that their school grades instead of increasing are in decline. FAILURE IN SCHOOL could be imminent. The BEHAVIOR CHANGE can be observed in them. Bullying victims have few or no friends and are often rejected because other children are afraid of being assaulted by perpetrators, and no longer want to join the victim.

Almost all of these children are aggrieved, suffer from anxiousness, loneliness, fear of participating in groups, insecurity that often extends to adulthood. SOME LOSE THEIR APPETITE AND OTHERS EAT TOO MUCH.

These children and teenagers drop out of school, and if they happen to be forced to finish high school, then they don't want to go to college for fear of being assaulted. Some children and/or adolescents have taken drastic measures against their lives. Just thinking about something like that hurts. It makes our heart tremble and our whole being chilling, and suffering, we have heard from families who have lost one of their members to bullying. Without any solution being sought for it so that this will not happen again. No family should suffer the loss of one of their own because they are victims of Bullying. Just by imagining all the suffering the victim has to go through, it tears. Too bad for the soul, quicken the heart, our whole being extremes. It produces sadness, a deep sorrow overwhelms us. Many see their future faded, they lose interest in moving on to a normal life.

Thousands of these young people start studying with big dreams, and then end up giving up because they are persecuted, intimidated by others.

It is necessary to put an end to this situation, so that no young person stops attending school and/or university out of fear. It is an inalienable right of all people to live in freedom. If he hasn't committed any crime that fights against the law and other good customs. Now is the time to turn on a light on the road to prevent bullying. Prevention in any situation plays an extremely important role. So that society may have healthy young people and tomorrow adults capable of living in it. Without them feeling the need to hurt anyone else. Children and young people who feel accepted, loved, protected, and secure. They will not feel the need to bully others, or physically assault them, when they know and are certain that at least one of their parents, family or another person offers them love. They generate less anxiety than those who are abandoned or lack care and supervision.

The guys who attack in most cases are. Or they have been the victims of some kind of violence, inside or outside their homes, something we don't know is tormenting them. They don't just suffer some consequences for bullying. They come dragging along an amalgam of difficulties and situations that they find very difficult to channel. They're victims of abuse or God knows what's happening to them. No one becomes an aggressor or violent without a prior situation that causes such action. Children are not born violent. We will have to investigate, why so many children and adolescents become aggressors and perpetrators. If you educate a child today, tomorrow you will not have to punish him or her, if we give them education at home, with love, with clear, established rules, if you teach them according to their age. Which things are allowed, and which are not? They will easily assimilate that there are lines and parameters that should not be crossed.

For example, when you're driving a car on the street, you don't cross it when the traffic light is red. They are capturing, and therefore learning. With affections far from aggressions, neither physical nor verbal according to their age that things are correct, and which are incorrect. But be careful without falling into rigidity, don't put, don't turn, don't pass, don't go through, don't twist, don't spin, don't talk, there comes a moment when they have only heard NO, NO, NO. In the long run, it will produce the same result as if they were not educated and cared for. Educate children with tolerance, understanding, and patience. Let them feel safe, free from hostility, when we train our children in a hostile home, the result will be a vile man.

We don't want a society full of hostile and spiteful people. Because in the end, society as a whole will end up paying dearly for the consequences.

As we all know, all good and bad actions in the short or long term leave their aftermath, some not so good and others disastrous; children and / or adolescents who do the Bullying to one or other boys. They don't do it just because they hurt you. That behavior has a reason why we don't know exactly, because each child is different from the others and the circumstances are equally different. Each situation will have to be investigated with caution, and according to the history and experiences of each child or adolescent. We would have to move a little further into the background to verify what is going on in the lives of those children or young people. Or perhaps we go further into the mother's pregnancy, she has probably been physically or psychologically abused. Who knows, maybe she did not have eat the necessary nutrients for her child to develop properly in her belly. Although these children are currently treating them well.

We'd have to look for everything that's happened since they were conceived. If at first glance it does not emerge why he or she assaults others. There will always be a cause; what causes a child or adolescent to bully another student. Regardless of who the aggressor is, a solution must be found to make it disappear from school and society in general. All those who provoke so many children and young people to attack their classmates verbally or physically.

Don't take a tree by its branches, the roots can't be seen. But they are the ones that allow the tree to grow.

If we look for the origin of the problem that is causing young people to behave out of the ordinary. By attacking some who they consider weak and vulnerable, we can guarantee that school bullying will disappear. The same will happen with those sequels of problems that arise from bullying.

The psychological effects and post-traumatic stress disorder are varied: digestive problems, fear, adjustment disorder, often have difficulty integrating into groups and a new school. These and other notable psychological and emotional effects leave victims traumatized and almost immobile. As a result, some of the victims find it difficult to socialize normally with others and integrate into society. No one says it will be easy to make society aware. To the world that bullying is a serious problem. That the right tools, resources and strategies should be sought; appropriate educational measures should be taken at home and in schools to prevent bullying. If the victims do not get the attention they deserve, there will always be perpetrators. More and more children and young people will be mentally and emotionally crippled, more families will continue to lose their children because of this terrible evil. All of us as a society can raise our voices against bullying. Work on finding and creating tools to make this problem disappear completely. Where the school environment becomes a place where children and young people feel safe, that their relatives do not have to carry out daily activities with the concern that their child may be disturbed or assaulted by one or more of their classmates. Let's raise our voices against bullying, never against the perpetrator. They are children who should be given help and some psychological treatment. As well as the victim, both should be treated by trained personnel. All this in favor of a better society for present and future generations.

PARENTS' ATTITUDES

It is very difficult for parents to know that their child is being bullied by one or more children and/or teens in school. Some of them probably feel helpless, not knowing what to do in the face of the situation. Some people wouldn't think twice about going after him or her, whether they were young or old, to go after him or her and ask them why the aggression against their son or daughter. Others would tell their children under threat, to defend themselves and not be humiliated unless they are beaten. We have heard from parents who have told their children that if they come home beaten I will be the one who will beat you up. they mustn't let anyone humiliate or beat them. There are those who would not ask the aggressors because it bothers their child, they simply take revenge in their hands. Serious error. Pretty expensive. They go themselves to attack whoever bothers their child, or girl. Others wait for them outside school and make them fight each other, further fomenting violence among boys. Without measuring the consequences of their actions and the conflict between the two families. And of course, they will have to face justice. All of these attitudes on the part of adults are wrong, wrong and unacceptable, negative beyond limits. Instead of fixing, it'll make the situation worse. No parent should go in search of the child aggressor, in short, is a child, waste of time, a problem more than the adult who does such a thing will face. In addition, multiple aggravating factors were added. No adult should attack children whether they are their children or not, all of these actions mentioned above are intolerable and unacceptable. Anyone who dares to make a decision of such magnitude will have to face serious consequences. They could enter a great dispute from which it would be difficult for them to get out. It is wrong to induce minors to take justice into their own hands. Nor encourage them to be violent. To urge them to resolve a situation with violence would make the situation much more complicated. At the end of the road both the father and his son will be harmed. No adult person will ever take retaliation against a minor, let alone influence his or her own to retaliate against someone who caused them harm, whether physical and/or emotional. Children and young people should be trained with a NO to violence. It's actually quite a difficult situation because we know it's not easy for anyone who has two fingers in front of them to know that they've assaulted their son or daughter and to stand still and do nothing about it. But urging minors to behave aggressively won't solve anything, it will only make the problem worse. Children must be educated for peace, a no to violence. It is important for them to grow up in healthy environments. There are a number of appropriate methods for resolving conflict, especially when it comes to school bullying. Some children and young people do not tell their parents and guardians what is happening to them at school or outside school, for fear of the attitude they might take. On several occasions, they do not speak because they may still receive threats from the aggressors. Or because of poor communication with parents, others are too busy and have no time to listen to their children.

Parents who don't get the least bit of space to know what's happening to their children at school. There are those who only go to the place where their children study if they misbehave and send for you. And another group that, even if they call them, never come forward and if for some reason they are suspended, they run to investigate and others that do not even form part of the school. There are different types of fathers and mothers. It's just that everyone will take care of and be attentive to everything that has to do with their children. Many are very responsible, and a few are not so responsible. The most reasonable thing would be for everyone to take a minimum amount of time to talk with their children about the day's events. The educational community is the one who must be in charge of calling both relatives who represent the minors, so that all together can reach some agreement and be able to resolve the problem. When certain parents, or relatives present some kind of violence, it would be advisable not to unite them, but to work with each family individually.

It will not be easy to reach a favorable agreement for the boys, both the victim and the perpetrator, who would normally have to think that something is not going very well in their life. Some internal or external problem is tormenting them to that of origin to a Bullying behavior. Once the young person, boy or girl feels intimidated and talks to their parents or because they have noticed any changes. The first step is to contact your child's school physicians. If he's not from school, the assailant. There it becomes more complicated because we will have to go in search of those responsible for that child or young person. When this happens, it would be advisable to be accompanied by a member or representative of the community to avoid verbal and physical aggression. You never know how people will react. Depending on who the parents of the victim and the perpetrator are, the solutions would be easy or very difficult. The attitude of the parents is very important when trying to solve a problem among minors. I met a family, when one of them went to tell the other family members to try to solve a Bullying problem with simple words that turned into physical aggressions among teenagers. Instead of finding a solution, it was aggravated by the fact that the adults ended up being beating each other. Among themselves, the end was disastrous. It will never be advisable to go to someone else's home under any pretext to seek a solution to a conflict between students. That's what the school is for, they know how to do it in the best way so that no more aggressions arise and a good solution to the dilemma shines through.

It is possible to find people who come to their senses trying to resolve the difficulty between the parties without anyone being affected. A friendly way out where bullying is stopped without anyone being hurt more, could be quite the opposite third parties could end up attacked and hostile families. Let us promote peace, harmony, among the children remembering that they and no one else are the future nations. They capture and observe what big people who are supposed to be role models are doing, they assimilate everything that surrounds them. Learning from the behavior of adults, family members, although on several occasions things get out of control. Not all variables can be handled.

Parents are not the only ones in the lives of children and young people, there is genetics. In addition to the family and school environment, they absorb a large number of information from which they assimilate and learn.

All a bombardment of information from the outside world very difficult to avoid.

Observation is a very good tool in verifying whether a child is being abused. Outside or on school grounds, teachers can also be vigilant because sometimes children are assaulted at home by adults. Most of them change the way they behave. Those who used to be happy, playful, funny, sociable, with no apparent cause become sad, distracted, distracted, sad, do not want to join with others, avoid leaving the house, although they will like school before. They lose interest, the motivation to attend and their grades are lower every day. Once a child begins to present these first symptoms, it is advisable to talk to him/her and in case he does not want to say anything, a thorough investigation at school is recommended. Talk to teachers, behavioral professionals, administrative staff and other school officials. It is the school that should talk to the parents of the abusers if they belong to it. Children who are assaulted are most likely to have symptoms of depression, poor appetite, lack of sleep, or overeating. Faced with any symptoms of depression you should immediately see a psychologist because he or she could fall into severe depression that would trigger major problems. A young bullying victim who does not have the right tools to solve such a situation. If you are not properly attended to by a staff with the proper preparation for your case. It could fall not only into severe depression, but also become isolated from the social world and more likely to fall into the use of prohibited substances. One way or another, bullying is a serious problem that destroys the integrity of the victim. Another fact that should not be overlooked is that a change of city, school, country, teachers, when they change classrooms, friends, and even when they start a new course can produce a change in behavior in children and adolescents. Even if they're not being bullying victims. All of the above could be a cause of instability in one child more than in others. Which would generate a possible change in his way of being and alter his behavior. That is why emphasis is placed on supervision and observation of minors. Different variables should be observed before concluding. If we want children and young people healthy physically and mentally, useful, act to live in a modern world in complete movement. Where every day that happens, things change. Nothing remains static. To build a society where future men and women are able to grow, achieving an optimal development in all aspects, free of violence. A yes to PEACE.

Educating them to be respectful men and women, capable of integrating themselves into society free from prejudice. True human beings who can live alongside diversity in any corner of the planet.

TEACHER'S ATTITUDES

There are many teachers who have had to face the ghost of bullying in school, while they have exercised their dignified and noble profession of being teachers; as we know is a job that everyone does in their lives.

They are worthy, however, that of being a teacher is out of the ordinary, they have great responsibility. The privilege, commitment, patience, vocation and love of forming all the boys, girls, men and women of society.

Who but them has had the divine and commendable work of not only to educate the past, present but also future generations? They, together with parents, are the creators, trainers of professionals. From their first beginnings until they finish their higher studies and insert themselves productively into the world of work. Teachers do their work with dedication and care. The truth is that they should be more recognized, respected, and admired. And of course, better paid, they are responsible, instructing, training all the small and large of our great ship called world.

With the same magnitude and honorability and responsibility to offer the bread of teaching. Educating all generations of the planet earth does not cease to have its advantages, disadvantages, sufferings and joys. It is a profession that offers satisfaction, enthusiasm and well-being, and a certain sadness, especially when it is realized by vocation. That intimate feeling of sowing seeds of knowledge, strengthening other people's minds with love but on various occasions. They are forced to deal with different types, situations and problems in school. It is very likely that some of them will get out of control when a boy, girl or adolescent presents any kind of problems of any kind, such as learning, family, or bullying. The first ones to suffer are the teachers, sometimes they spend a lot of time with the students, there are many places where the students, saddened, go home. And those who, in addition to educators, become protectors, format-ters, defenders, friends, and on various occasions must even take on the role of parents without their children.

For a teacher, that a student becomes a victim of bu-llying is difficult for them, in addition to having a student who isolates itself, they are distracted; they leave the class-room when their body remains there, but their mind walks elsewhere.

They don't share with the group. He doesn't share with the group. He doesn't want to go to recess. He gets depres-sed, even if he has been a good student, his grades will go down, there is the possibility that if he is not attended to quickly neglected by abandoning his studies. People who have chosen to be teachers as a trade or profession exercise it with joy, devotion, motivation and enthusiasm. But they suffer. They get grief when one of their students does not respond adequately as they should. And what if the perpe-trator is still one of yours. Grief and sadness multiply. Two problems arise in your classroom, to which you must find a quick solution before it spreads. His suffering is now worth two and may end up multiplying. Depending on how many students are involved, as we can observe the task of being a teacher, it is a great challenge. It's not as easy or as beautiful as it seems. It requires responsibility, someone may believe that it has the fragrance and color of roses, even they have thorns. It is a profession of great commitment, although it leaves its high degree of satisfaction.

When they can see those young people, who have trained and realized their dreams come true, there is no doubt that their happiness is imminent.

The other side of the coin, the hardest to look at is that some of his own have not achieved the necessary gains. Both inside and outside the classroom because they have been victims of bullying, simply because they are victims or perpetrators. Many of the victimizing children and adolescents almost always stop studying. They drop out of school because they are unable to meet the standards set in school or because the school is forced to suspend them. Because of his behavior, other schools won't want to receive him either, we should look for a solution, so that some teacher can teach him at home. But isolation is not convenient, though perhaps necessary. Applying a time-out technique will benefit you, having effect while modifying your behavior, provided you receive treatment by a psychologist or trained staff. Until they can go back to school again.

The teacher knows very well that beyond that child or young offender there is a situation. Who knows if it's family problems, that is manifesting through bullying. There may be some conflict in the student that teachers are unaware of, but they know something is wrong with him or her.

However, while the student remains in his or her classroom, the solutions would be much easier for both the victim and the perpetrator. When they remain in school, it is much easier to work with both victim and offender.

Early intervention by teachers in this case could achieve a friendlier solution for both sides by working in the company of parents and all school staff. A teacher can almost never solve a problem of this magnitude on his own, because far from finding a good way out, it could be difficult for him.

As a general rule, parents should be aware of any difficulties their children are going through, their help and cooperation in the process of education, teaching their children how to learn is essential. The teacher's involvement once the first signs of verbal aggression are visible. Or bullying through gestures among their students. Talk to him or her privately, with the intention of stopping the Bullying against his or her partner. Keeping in mind that any problem with students deserves to be followed up, in the short or long term. Information to parents is essential, it should never be ignored.

The situation should not be expected to get too complicated to talk to those responsible for the children; a day of waiting may be too late. The first and most important step is to communicate with both parents to make them aware of what is happening with their children. Both those of the aggressor and the assailant are obliged to appear. It may be the case that some parents do not respond to the call for lack of time. They are not in the country, they have no interest in the school life of their son, daughter, or because they are no longer there. Here the teacher will be a little more complicated because he or she will have to call the people with whom the students live. Almost never the children live alone, there will always be an adult to represent them, that is precisely what you should seek to inform the situation. Together, teachers, the school community and/or parents and guardians will need to join forces to stop verbal aggression and not reach other levels. No teacher should take revenge in their hands when a student is physically, verbally or psychologically assaulted. Even if the victim is one of your best students or a relative. When it comes to problems among students in any school, no matter what, or where they are. Teachers should not take it personally, they are all students whether they are their own or not, no teacher should be biased one way or the other. All students deserve equal treatment, fairness is part of the solution. Neither should parents take it personally. In no way can a conflict between students be brought to an end, and for no reason should parents go to him or her or the aggressors for redress. It should be thorough teamwork, school community, including a behavioral professional or trained staff that should not be left out, because it is they and the parents who should find the tools to solve the problem. And to manage to modify the abuser's behavior in the company of the parents, and for more than enough reasons these last parents and guardians who of course must be present whenever their children have a problem are victims or perpetrators. Parents should never be left out, nor should they be strangers to all that is happening with their greatest treasures, their children. The greater the participation of parents in their children's school development and process, the less difficult the work of teachers would be. The cooperation of parents in the school process of their children will facilitate school work. The more parents get involved in their children's school life, the less trouble there will be in society and therefore the future of young people would be more guaranteed in the end parents would benefit the most. They will be able to sing victory and the teachers will be more satisfied with their work, in the same way they will be offering society people who are more and more integrated and who in turn will be forming new generations. Working, parents, teachers and society together so that generations to come can live in violence-free homes. Don't let it spread through time. Households should be the first to be given zero tolerance for abuse, physical, verbal, mental and psychological abuse.

THE DEADLY WEAPON CALLED BULLYING

Bullying in general is a problem that has always existed. But that over time has become a great difficulty. A problem that has harmed many adolescents in one way or another, wrapping up numerous families, leaving them seriously injured and even lost.

We have observed that when a dangerous disease appears worldwide, solutions are being sought to stop the disease and that fewer people are affected by the epidemic or pandemic. But when it comes to school bullying, though certain sectors have worked timidly, and some people and institutions have not given up hope that more families will lose one or more of their members, because they are victims of this terrible problem. Greater attention needs to be paid to it. In addition to the human losses we have suffered for this cause, some have been emotionally weakened with their lives torn to pieces. If adequate solutions are not sought in time, it could still become a social pandemic, which will continue to claim more victims. Many young people and children have apparently died from bullying. In fact, it has become a social problem, it has not been one or two young people who are not with their loved ones now because they have suffered this terrible nightmare falling into severe depression, all because someone else did Bullying. It is very likely that there are no truly established statistics to identify an exact number of all the victims who have not been able to recover from this problem today.

The truth is that many families today do not have any family. Because bullying, as if it were a deadly disease, takes them from their family's bosom. If someone is no longer with his own, because he got sick, it is very hard and painful, but it is less difficult to accept it and recover from the pain. Suffering is most profound and devastating when a family loses a member of their family to this terrible misnamed Bullying.

What to say about what they are not with their families now, because the Bullying took him away from the family environment. Others in social life or have simply seen their dreams cut short by fear or fear of throwing themselves into the real world for being a victim. Not only in schools but also at home, because some people have not had to go to school to make fun of them. There are families that cause pain and suffering to their children by labeling and naming them, end up hurting them and hurting them until they are older.

Bullying can become a deadly and dangerous weapon if the right tools are not sought so that fewer children, adolescents and even adults are emotionally mutilated. Because of this problem, even more so if they are family members. Those who suffer most and are affected by bullying are teenagers between the ages of twelve and seventeen. At the high school stage, this is a very serious problem that must be addressed quickly. Let's join our efforts to look for tools aimed at prevention, stopping bullying, as it has become a situation that concerns everyone, is not a simple school problem and simple human lives are being lost. Our children and adolescents who suffer for this cause, even if the victim is not known. It hurts to know that something like this is killing people who are undoubtedly our greatest treasures. Although today they are children and adolescents, the most vulnerable part of society, they must be cared for and protected as the future. Any problem in their lives slows them down, academically and emotionally, bullying has become a bleak picture. A situation that seems to be typical of schools but has become a social issue.

There could be a kind of psychological death, anxiety, sadness, low esteem and a series of triggers. That is not with a good intervention and an effective therapeutic treatment with a well-trained psychologist.

Maybe the victim isn't in a position to be superimposed for the rest of her life.

The most effective medicine against school bullying is not sold in pharmacies. Neither in any store given or to be had, the remedy is only in homes. Wherever in the world there is a home, where there are children and/or adolescents. That's where you can start putting the Bullying prevention tools in place.

Where we can find the primary healing pill to prevent, end school bullying, let's start with the first family society. Nothing and no one is more important to a child or adolescent than their relatives.

The right place to start cutting the root of Bullying, who have had the privilege of having these great treasures, which do not only belong to them, belong to society. However, each one is responsible for the sons and daughters that God lends them. For while they enjoy that precious and beautiful privilege, for they do not all have it, and others who have been given it have rejected it. But to whom God has given the joy of being a pregnant or adopted father and mother, they have the duty. Not only to provide them with clothes and food, sincere, unconditional affection, care, attention and above all communication with children are necessary, to offer them a home where they feel loved, protected, safe, and accepted. A home free of abuse, offenses, name-calling, or labels, only some merchandise should be labeled. Others do not need them, and the ones that wear them are only to identify the manufacturer or owner of the brand.

The sweetest and most beautiful melody anyone can hear is their name, call it by its name; stop telling them that they are stupid, they are good for nothing; TO CHANGE THE DISCOURSE, NOT JUST IN A HOME, EVERYWHERE, TELL THEM THAT THEY ARE IMPORTANT, THAT THEY ARE GOOD, INTELLIGENT, THAT THEY WILL ACHIEVE GREAT ACHIEVEMENTS WHEN THEY ARE GROWN UP, THAT YOU CAN ALWAYS ACHIEVE IT. You have to tell them that even if they're small, they can still dream. Urge them to have dreams. Support them so that they can reach them. Don't let anyone attack them, don't support labels or name calling. When someone hurts your children, it's as if they hurt their own person. Because in short, it was you and no one else who got this wonderful loan to be a parent. I'm sure that if someone is given a loan of money in a bank that person who has received it will not want to spend it on superfluous things, but on the most important ones, on their priorities. Those are the children, priorities. Give them time, even if you can't afford it, give them quality time, make them feel safe and secure. All the above mentioned among some other tools that can be used so that Bullying, not to continue being that destructive weapon that has entered the schools, putting an end to the emotional peace of children, young people and of course the family.

That the lack of a responsible adult does not create a vacuum in the interior of their being, their mind. Here, the priorities are and always will be children and adolescents, they are the future of society as a whole. Let us work in the first school, the universal one, which must lay the main foundations of a child's existence. Yours, everyone's, the main education begins at home. With the people they have first contact with. They should not leave the family education of their sons and daughters to school, to teachers, the role of teachers is different, each has the responsibility and duty to play their part. It's not fair for teachers to have to carry a suitcase that doesn't belong to them because it's not theirs. You can cooperate, but in your role as a teacher. The fact is that some parents settle in, leaving the schools and their staff a task that belongs to them as parents. The school system plays an extremely important role in the life and academic development of students. But that of parents and guardians should not be weakened under any circumstances.

Even when children are in school, the work of parents should continue to send their children to school does not exempt those primarily responsible for their physical, mental and emotional health. And in particular, you should help them with their homework. Building homes, free of violence, verbal, physical and psychological. But EYE, true homes, not a house to house them, without any supervision, protection or care, where love, respect and understanding and communication are conspicuous by their absence, no great effort or power to buy is needed. The most important things they need the money can never be bought. They need the presence of their parents, love, attention, good communication, human sensitivity, tolerance, patience, homes where values are present, no violence. What makes children and adolescents grow up confident.

It has nothing to do with whether their parents have positions or not. They also feed them clothes, shoes, and electronic games. All of the above favors them. Whatever technology helps them in their intellectual development, allows them to develop skills, increase their potential, acquire different skills. But they require and want loving parents who make them feel safe, not overprotective. That they do not allow them to grow as healthy social entities, so that they do not become victims or perpetrators. A good foundation in the home from an early age. It could be a very good tool to start fighting bullying in schools. And above all, to allow them to speak, to communicate when something is happening to

them, to learn to defend their rights peacefully, through dialogue. Love is the most powerful weapon in the world. It can
put an end not only to bullying, it is capable of transforming
human beings, making them sensitive, courageous, compas-
sionate, supportive, tolerant patients. Treating children and
adolescents with love will make them worthy men and women and act to live in any society.

However, parents should not allow strangers to label
their children. No matter whoever it is, whoever tries or does
it. This is also a good step towards stopping this problem. In
reality, it could be that this problem can sometimes get out
of hand. Not because of lack of attention and care by adults,
but because children and young people are in contact with
a series of extra-family information, which sometimes become uncontrollable. A constant and hard work is required.
Even if parents seek the best care for their children, the situation may be complicated. Because, in addition to the home,
children and young people are exposed to the environment
outside the home. Many well-taken care of children, with a
very good education and whose parents and guardians have
stripped themselves of themselves to dedicate their lives to
caring for their children. They face the crossroads that their
children are not perpetrators. But they become the victim of
someone else who has not received the same care. And that
they may have had to live in shaky, dysfunctional, abusive,
or very permissive homes, not because they have chosen that
way of living, but because unfortunately that is what they
have had to face. This is when schoolwork gets heavier, harder and more complicated. Because in one way or another
whoever the child is must be helped. And without the proper
involvement of a responsible adult, it is often complicated
by further efforts by the school community that the work
done will not be able to achieve the desired goal. Good supervision of parents, not only with regard to the daily life
of their children, but also with regard to responsibility and

active presence in school work. They must be accompanied during their academic life while they are minors. Let the parents, even when they are separated, maintain good communication with their sons and daughters, because after all they are the parents and no one else. In case they divorce, let it be between them, that they do not divorce their children, that they do not emotionally involve the children and/or adolescents in their conflicts because this causes them pain, anxiety, worry and insecurities. Becoming irritable, bullying, or shy may affect your mental health and academic performance at school. It is the parent's responsibility to remain alert, observing any behavioral changes in their child's behavior, whether it is a child and/or adolescent. Several indicators could reveal that he or she is going through some difficulty. Whether it's bullying or not, for example: when you don't want to eat, or you eat excessively, when you used to feed in moderation before, it's very likely that some source of anxiety is invading you and there must be a possible cause. They no longer feel any interest or desire to go to school. They don't play. They prefer to lie at home sleeping for several hours without any apparent physical illness, they are dissatisfied, irritable, or on the contrary submissive, very calmly lower their grades, when a child presents a demotivation in relation to school and their homework. It is necessary to investigate what situation is causing this change, talk with the doctor, to know if there is any physical problem, a psychologist or other licensed and competent professional. Before the situation gets even more complicated. All of these small steps will help detect whether children or adolescents are being bullied at school or elsewhere.

One lady told me that one of her children bullied her at school because she was a bit heavier than the others in her classroom. He's always been overweight since he was very young. Every day he went to school, his classmates teased him just because he was overweight. The child did not want to attend school. His mother carried him every day, motivating him as she did with his two siblings, a girl and another little boy.

They were in the same school, but the Bullying victim. He hid out, so he wouldn't go to school. He made all sorts of excuses not to attend with fear to the teasing of other children just because of his weight. One day she was carrying him, he let go of her hands and ran down a street. His worried mother looked all over the place for several hours until she found him in a hidden clothing store. That day she didn't take him to school, because he begged her. Crying, he didn't want to go, so she went to school to see what was going on with her son.

And she also asked him why he refused to go to his school. When his brothers did not complain and were always ready to attend. She, a mother completely dedicated to the care and well-being of her children, was deeply concerned about her second child's problem. That day that got out of hand, she left him at home. It was she who went to school to talk to the teacher about what was going on. The next day she took her son to her classroom with anxiety and worry that he might run away again. And for all the reasons she had to take him to school. Children should not be left at home, and she had to work to support them. Because the father was also absented from the home. They were separated and when they lived together anyway, he was just there to say he was. And to assault her verbally, all the weight of the household and the children were on the Lord's shoulders. That was only the reflection of so many other cases in society. A few more days passed, and the boy complained again about not wanting to go to school with his siblings, the mother proposed changing him from school so that he wouldn't be there. But he was very afraid to go to anyone else with the fear of being a Bullying victim. She decided to go to the same school, but the lady had to go to work to help them prepare. She would prepare breakfast for them, like the other siblings, take them to school and then go to work. But with anxiety, stress and worry that he might not get in, he would go out for his school. But he wouldn't go in. For that reason, she decided to leave them in front of the school. But the boy stayed close until the hours passed. He didn't have a grade, until she was called from school to let them know he wasn't attending. After a long time of struggle, the mother could do nothing. With all the effort she made, however, the boy did not want to return to school. He dropped out of the studies and painfully immersed himself in the use of prohibited substances.

We may not be able to avoid children and young people who are exposed to the difficulties of life. Because isolating them from the environment, preventing them from having relations with everything that goes with living in the world would be a mistake that would end up hurting them even more. They should be given the opportunity to confront the spines and spider webs from outside. That is the real world, there are stones and stumbles that in short, only serve to shape the character of people. We're not going to lock them up, like another mother I met in my office. She wouldn't let her daughter meet anyone. She educated her at home, as a teacher she was in charge of teaching the child. Without attending school, the clothes he was allowed to wear were out of fashion. Some horrible dresses that I was forced to suggest she change her dress. Because it was inappropriate for her age. The lady accepted the suggestions as good and valid. She gave up her wrong way of educating and dressing her preteens and didn't know what it meant to have friends because her mother wouldn't let her. Children need to relate to other children is how they socialize with their peers and their environment. In this way, they are strengthened psychologically and mentally. In addition to their family they require friends and classmates. Life will not always be rosy.

Even roses are very beautiful, but they have thorns. They need to learn to face the difficulties of life, that falling and rising from difficulties. And to live in a world full of falls and stumbles, is that it prepares them to be strong and able to face any situation that arises. Let's imagine a little plant whatever it is. That we keep it locked up, where it doesn't get the light and heat of the sun. It will not be strong enough to withstand the brunt of a hurricane wind. While if we leave it exposed to the sun and rain, its roots will become stronger and in this way, such a plant would have a better chance of surviving in the face of any storm or other natural phenomenon. In this way, children become stronger and learn when they are in the company of other children.

Children and young people should be trained so that when someone wants to harm them, they have the strength and capacity not to let themselves be overwhelmed. And neither should we succumb, before the attacks and problems. Whether it is bullying or any other difficulty, let us work to offer children and young people a strong and healthy mind so that when someone wants to do bullying they can defend themselves, without resorting to violence. Let them tell their elders, teachers and parents at school what is happening to them. Don't be afraid to talk to your parents. The latter are the ones who must defend themselves, without any kind of violence towards other children. Children raised in homes with a strong foundation and clear rules. With a vast values-based education, when faced with a problem of any kind they are able to get over it faster.

May they be allowed to live and develop in homes where love, tolerance, understanding and acceptance reign, where they feel appreciated and encouraged. That they can believe, have faith, that they are just, respectful, kind, honest, how beautiful. Wonderful would be that in every home on the planet Earth, where there are children and adolescents, they would feel wanted, safe, loved, and protected.

With all these and more, there is no such thing as bullying in school. There will be no hardship in the world that will make any of our children and/or adolescents suffer. To motivate children and young people, to urge them to overcome all the barriers that appear in the path of life.

Educate them with a strong enough mind. All of this would serve to prevent and thus diminish the statistics of those who do Bullying, and as a consequence there will be no victim. When children are happy and feel that their relatives love and respect them and allow them to express themselves freely. They will not want to disturb others, because they are happy and satisfied, let us build a better world for future leaders and all future generations.

EDUCATION IN VALUES

It's true that most things go out of fashion, a new orchestra displaces another one that emerges later and gets stuck, a song gets a prominent place in the radio stations occupying the first places in the world until BOOM. Another one emerges that impresses the public, taking it out of the way. It's almost the same with fashion, clothes and shoes, auto, as well, as designers. They create a new piece that grabs the shops, and everyone buys them, there comes a time when no one cares anymore, and they prefer what is at the last shout. However, there are many treasures that, no matter how old they may be and although time has passed, they never go out of fashion. Perhaps a little forgotten, those treasures are human values, although it is possible that in each society they have their own values.

To cultivate values, it is proper of each individual, it is a right of each one to live in the form and the way he wishes. However, households that care for them and put them into practice in their children's education over time have managed to train men and women who are more adaptable to the precepts and norms of society.

Today, as in the past, there are many homes all over the world. Where these great treasures have not been left aside, human values, they do not go out of fashion like other things, they are still there, we only have to go to their inexhaustible source. This source of positive things that would serve as the basis for homes, an important platform to promote a solid family education.

When we make use of human values we all gain, if we start with respect, wherever there is this value it is very difficult to create sources of aggression against someone. If

we teach children early on with examples, this precious treasure, children are taught to no, with words and actions, the
first step is to respect their rights. Once they realize that their
children are respected, they will understand that they must
respect their parents, siblings and other people's belongings,
they will learn that other children's toys do not belong to
them and therefore must respect them. But never a child who
is not respected will know that they must.

Tolerance is not an easy task to educate and raise a child
until he or she becomes independent from his or her parents or guardians. But this is a beautiful privilege that not
all people have, even if they wanted to, whoever God has
given them that great gift. You must be tolerant, and cultivate patience, because children are those children. They will
learn from the environment around them if they grow up in
a home with intolerant, hostile, violent and abusive adults,
with rare exceptions;

They will learn to be inflexible, an environment plagued
with rigidity does not favor the children, and/or adolescent,
but there are also the other extreme extremely flexible homes where there are no clear rules of coexistence. Both situations will only be to the detriment of minors, there must
be a balance when it comes to educating children. They need
models for learning, but without the rules going to either
end. Learning that they do not live alone in the world, that
there are more human beings and other living beings to be
respected, and if possible being within our reach to care and
protect. The responsibility for educating children in family
education does not lie with school, but with the family. But
many times, they don't have time available, so many adult
responsibilities and commitments.

Since there are some variables that cannot be controlled.
Implementing human values in the academic curriculum

could be favorable, so that children absorb good manners and some values from the beginning of school. Such as respect, comradeship, solidarity, kindness, kindness, tolerance, justice, integrity, honesty, honesty, sincerity, righteousness, friendship, solidarity, loyalty and a series of values that exist and far from harming children. It will help to ensure that your character and personality are properly shaped. If they are taught from an early age, when they reach adolescence we will have a large part of the journey. Aggression may diminish even when they have been touched, living in homes devoid of sensitivity, humility, firmness, love, understanding and values.

It's still time, not everything is lost, let's all work together to end up with Bullying at school, the first stone must start at home, if we want to build a strong house that can withstand the biggest storms. You must start by laying a strong and adequate foundation, so that it does not collapse with a simple breeze.

Train children so that when someone attacks them they have the strength. Strength and courage not to let themselves be harmed, intimidated or succumbed, who are able to communicate the first sign of verbal aggression. Confidence in being able to talk to parents, teachers or anyone at home, at school. And may their mental strength allow them to overcome the adversities of the environment. That they do not feel motivated to solve problems that in one way or another arise in the lives of human beings, that do not resort to aggression.

Nor to violence, without affecting them, and so they can succeed in any situation that may arise inside and outside the school, without having to violate the rights of others. Don't become aggressors or victims. A good upbringing in values forms good morals and character to such a high degree that when they reach adulthood, they are able to insert themselves in society, authentic and properly. To inculcate human values from the very first years of life so that they become their own as they grow. Later on, they are in charge of promoting this lifestyle in the next generations. The goal is not to tell a person how to educate his or her child, nor to impose parameters on them, but the family that educates with values has a greater chance of having children who respect other's rights. Even if some things get out of hand, they have already planted the seed, over time it will grow as a small plant does; in the end fruits can be collected. It is known that each culture has its own values, yet good manners and good customs will never go out of fashion as other things happen. Recover values, instilling them in children from an early age. It would be a good tool to prevent school bullying.

A DIFFICULT TASK

The task of making Bullying disappear at school is not as easy as going to a store and buying a garment. Because even if it joins all the efforts made and for having, it is like a plant with deep roots, even if they are cut, there are always sprouts, around them, that seem to be a difficult task; to finish with those small plants that have been left. But good care, commitment, hard work and effective, if only in the long run, would end these harmful outbreaks. Of course, if it is possible, each of us paying a small fee, with only one purpose: to stop violence and aggressions against children, and among the children, supervision, care, protection, discipline without violence, neither physical nor verbal, and much less psychological, discipline will never be synonymous with aggression of any kind, affection and affection. Everything they need to develop as a healthy individual that is not replaced by a lot of material things, which are very good, necessary and important. As long as they are not used to fill an affective void, which if not properly filled will always be dormant. All the material that can be offered to a child is propitious, good and wonderful, as long as it is not intended to replace the valuable quality time and love that they require their parents or guardians to provide.

All the material that can be bought from children is necessary to be able to live, in this competitive world, it is favorable that they grow at the same time of technological advances. Whatever technology is, of course, supervised will be of great help to them in their intellectual development. In addition to a good diet and family education, they should be offered homes where they feel loved, protected and taken to the doctor to know that they are in good health. Support them with their homework, recreation, fun and a series of other things that serve as tools for them to grow up healthy

as children, to be taught their homework. But without violating their rights, let them be respected. Children need to be
listened to, by their parents, they need to be aware of who
their friends are and what they do in their company. All of
the above accompanied by good supervision by the parents
and/or guardians programs that their minor children watch
through social networks. And most of all television, as far
as possible to be supervised, in almost every home there is
a television, a computer, a table, a mobile phone. But it is
the parents who are responsible for this work, no outsider
should intervene in the family education of children. When
children and/or adolescents are hit as victims of bullying,
external wounds heal. But the intern is very difficult to cure,
sometimes they stay for life or become indelible traces.

Helping to prevent, stop, reduce and eradicate bullying
in the school environment, violence among students, promoting a chain of instruments. Creating all the tools, given
and to be had: as are the educational programs at social level
could contribute.

Even so, it is the parents who must look after their welfare and watch over what they do, what they watch and with
whom their children meet. Use all available means and resources to prevent and stop bullying at school. The problem
is that as long as there are outbreaks of domestic violence, it
becomes more difficult.

All of us as a society have a duty to offer children and
young people a better future and say that in union there is
strength. it's time to join forces to educate our children, to
guide one that other parents, if necessary, are not all prepared
to face and manage these problems, and many need guidance
to help their children become good and better citizens. Looking for all the tools at your fingertips, all united to contribute a grain of sand, cooperate in the identification, prevention,

arrest and elimination of this problem that hurts us, hurts and lacerations the soul, even when the victim is not someone we know. To hear that a person is a young child or adult ended his life because of this terrible evil is quite painful. Other times it is the case that it is not the victim who has ended their life, the aggressions go so far that someone ends up with the victim's existence. Other times the same jaded victim of so much bullying feels cornered and decides to attack the perpetrator. The victim ends up being the aggressor, there have been horrible cases where those who were intimidated tuck in their despair and decide not to put up with any more intimidation. Some make regrettable decisions and others, even if they continue to live, are psychologically crippled.

Unless they do not receive effective therapeutic treatment, they cannot get out of this terrible problem. It is very likely that Bullying has not been given the attention it requires. This is the time, the moment that Bullying begins to be seen as what it is, a problem that ends with peace, tranquility, annihilates emotionally and ends with the existence of the victim. It is time to give it the importance it deserves, to confront it as what it really is, dangerous and destructive. When dealing with children and adolescents, quick and effective solutions must be found; they do not think about consequences. For this reason, adults should look for possible solutions to stop school bullying.

Such a situation is embarrassing, it is painful to hear the ridicule that dehumanized people make towards children even for having a special condition.

It does not matter if the person being bullied is a child, adolescent or adult. That's not fair. This situation should not continue, who is fortunate enough to know what inconvenience the person has had that day, and despite what is happening to them in their life, also has to endure the jokes that make them tormented, with ridicule or intimidation. It seems to be very difficult to eradicate these undesirable behaviors that are increasing every day that passes by, at a gigantic rate as a destructive phenomenon, to the detriment not only of the victim, but also of his family.

The family is responsible for stopping in the middle of so many activities that adults have to devote a little quality time to children. In addition to offering the parents peace of mind, it will allow them to enjoy their childhood, as they grow up quite fast. If the parents are neglected, when they want to pay attention and care sometimes it is a little late, it gets out of hand. By the time he realizes it, they've grown and grown up, those beautiful moments of sharing with his children vanish like the wind.

Who is he who is so bold that he can run after the wind to stop it, no matter how fast it may run and even if he had wings, it would not reach him.

That's what happens with children, if you don't take advantage of them when they are young to educate them in homes with a good family education, there's no time at the end.

And in case this enormous task is left to the school, although it is true that a good education in values at an academic level could help, without forgetting that every society is different. Bearing in mind that what could be a value for a society may not work elsewhere. Although values and good manners, good behavior would never be superfluous anywhere. A sustainable family education would be the best foundation when combating outbreaks of violence is about the education provided by schools and teachers. Academically speaking, it is necessary and important, but the latter needs to have the foundations of a family education, so that there is a better and more balanced balance between the two.

Households are the first major school in any country in the world. It is for this reason that it is the responsibility of the family to provide quiet, peace, well-being and tranquility to their children. It seems to be a difficult task, to put an end to bullying, not obstructing if we work as a family, school and society with the purpose that this evil that has destroyed and emotionally damaged children and adolescents; seek an effective solution and follow it up.

All together we can contribute to the decrease of violence and bullying in schools, which has become a problem that if we don't look for the appropriate and quick tools to prevent, treat and stop it, it will be out of control. We must all cooperate to give a no' vote to school bullying, to give it a stop sign, before more lives are lost. It is not enough to look from afar at a situation that is damaging our greatest treasures. Putting aside does not lead to any safe place, an effective and arduous work between all parties is required if we want to build a society where everyone can live in peace without exception.

School bullying requires the commitment of society as a whole to prevent, stop and eradicate bullying, even when it is a difficult task. We all have the power to stop a problem that is leaving so much damage and destruction in our childhood and adolescence. Let's start at home by teaching them to respect the principles and values of others. It is the main formula and the only way to live together in harmony.

With others, and in the midst of so much diversity.

BULLYING AFFECTS US ALL

Bullying has become a problem that is harmful to our children, adolescents and therefore to society itself.

The activities inside the classroom once there is a victim are no longer the same. The motivation to learn and enthusiasm of students will never be the same. Worse even when they are both in the same classroom. Verbal and non-verbal threats affect not only the victim, but other children are sometimes affected.

A Bullying situation serves as a distraction for all those present to divert their attention easily, the concentration is lost, the academic performance of students could be in decline. If control is not maintained, one way or another the school environment is disrupted. When it comes to teenagers, it is sometimes more complicated because some join the perpetrators. Those who disagree with the violence isolate themselves from the victim, for fear of being assaulted, the victim ends up without friends. Not for lack of socialization, but rather because other children reject them out of fear of being other victims. Sometimes they receive direct threats from the perpetrator. In these cases, the role of the teacher has to play a very important role, but it requires the participation of the principals and of course the parents. When it comes to children and young people, nothing can be achieved without the presence of their parents or the people responsible for them, it is hard work and therefore together, to look for possible solutions. The best ones aimed at helping both the victim and the perpetrator, he or she who at times are victims of another situation within or outside their family environment. To stop verbal aggression. And before they reach physical violence, the corrective measures must be on time and effective, the best thing to do is to avoid and of course not to resort to any kind of violence, neither psychological, verbal or even less physical to correct the kids. These will make them more aggressive, it is known that aggression generates more aggression, using violence to correct them, the only thing that will be achieved is that they become more violent, and rebellious. To treat them and apply the appropriate corrective measures for each case. The intervention of behavioral professionals would give excellent results, for treatment in these cases are psychologists. It is important that both victims and perpetrators receive psychological help. The victim should receive effective treatment, but the perpetrator should not be left out. He or she also needs to be treated, otherwise the levels of violence will not go down.

Parent involvement will always be necessary. That they commit themselves to actively participate in this process for a better effectiveness, seeking the well-being of their children. If you want to correct a child or there are thousands of methods, without resorting to verbal violence. Aggressions through gestures should never be used. Sometimes children are only seeking care from their parents or guardians who resort to inappropriate behavior to get the care they need.

If a child does not have any organic, physical or psychological problems that alter their behavior. It is very likely that you are only looking to be cared for, loved and protected.

Other times are learned behaviors, children living in hostile homes, where verbal and physical and non-verbal assaults. They are the bread and butter of every day, it is here where the situation is complicated because, although in school the children are helped, the problem is deeper. Working with violent individuals often complicates the situation, requiring hard work, professionalism, ethics, and a lot of patience to get parents to change aggressive behaviors against their children.

It won't be an easy task, but not an impossible one, you have to start, if you don't start threshing a path, you will never be able to walk along it. To get to a place it is necessary to know where you want to get to and take the first step, nobody dares to climb a ladder up the last step, you must start by taking the first step in the first. For bullying behavior to disappear from school, good parent involvement is essential. The school alone can do nothing, the active and effective presence of the family is the main basis for this problem to be prevented, stopped and/or eradicated from school, from homes. Extinguishing bullying in all its ramifications could take time, although in the long term it is necessary to work so that it ends, that there are no victims or perpetrators. No child or adolescent should feel insecure or afraid of attending school, children should not live in fear, this prevents them from growing and developing as an individual, as a person and integrating properly into society.

All together we can cooperate not only to stop this problem, to work so that the next generations do not have to suffer because they are victims of Bullying, and so that this problem is totally eradicated once and for all from the schools.

Education leads to a path of freedom, educating our children and adolescents so that they learn to live in harmony, in peace, with themselves, with nature, with respect, towards others, towards diversity and that they can comply with and keep the rules of society.

EFFECTIVE CORRECTION

A s already mentioned in previous chapters, Bullying is the intimidation that someone receives without apparent physical, mental, verbal, and/or psychological motive that an individual does against the victim. There is no apparent reason, because in most cases the victim does not have any rose with whom they do the bullying, nor has it caused them wrong, who becomes a victim. At other times, the victim only becomes an easy prey, so that someone will cause him/her discomfort, almost always begins with verbal attack, gestures, mental and psychological, but most likely it will reach physical aggression. Bullying, although it appears mostly in the school, there are several places where the spotlights appear. We will start by applying the possible corrective measures, in the first society, the family, because it is the main place that receives the children and therefore. She provides them with the first care from birth and protects them and cares for them during the early years that are the ones that will most influence the development of their personality. It is in the family bosom where children begin to have their first contact and it is precisely at home that they begin their most intimate interaction. These early years will not only be decisive but will also play a vital role in its future development. Bearing in mind that they do not necessarily have to be parents, many children live with a family group that does not possess a bloodline connection, yet children are cared for, loved, protected, educated, properly educated.

And they have the opportunity to grow in favorable environments. Even though the bonds that unite them are not blood ties, they are united by love and all the pleasant and positive things that come from that unconditional love that independent children should receive if they are our blood children, adopted or pregnant. It is important to know that children need correction when engaging in behavior that is out of the ordinary, but ATTENTION, an effective correction, used to teach them not to repeat it. Free of offenses, broken words, and as a rule physical abuse should be eradicated once and for all, children do not learn when they are abused. These outdated methods must be eliminated, unless you want to have future men and women who are spiteful, bitter, hostile and abusive. Teenagers become rebellious when they are treated with aggression, even if only simple gestures are used. The little ones become sad, anxious and anxious children, they think that their parents or guardians do not accept them, they do not want them. No child should feel that kind of sensation. Ideally, all of them should grow up happily and joyfully feeling loved, protected, supported, desired. If we apply these simple corrective measures in the home, we will surely be laying the first foundations to prevent, stop, and of course eradicate bullying. Communication at home is extremely important for children to be afraid, not afraid to talk about a difficulty they are going through. It is not in the best interests of isolating minors from the outside world because this same world outside of them. It provides them with the necessary tools to develop themselves

Socially and psychologically, it is necessary that they learn to grow and live with all the difficulties of life itself. Children cannot be removed from the outside to protect them from bullying or other bullying. The right thing would be to prepare them to learn to live in a world that sometimes becomes a little difficult, to strengthen their self-esteem.

By the time they go outside, they can get as unharmed as possible from the hardships that might arise along the way. Recognizing that there are variables beyond the reach not only of adults, but also of children; Fellowship, harmony, tolerance, peace. Solidarity, friendship, love of neighbor and a series of human values that exist and are there, are things that we must inculcate in the minds of children and above all respect for ourselves and others, including all living beings. The downside is that children and teens will not take any of this seriously if they don't notice that people who were born before they, did not. They learn more from examples than simple words. There is no way for a behavior to disappear, first if it is reinforced and second if children grow up looking at someone who does it. They are learning from all those who can perceive their environment, they need models, especially in their homes. Without forgetting all the others in the outside world around them, which has some influence on their behavior. As long as it is corrected with love, without violence of any kind. They who are still children will know how to take good adult behaviors, effective correction has nothing to do with abuse by those who are taking care of the children. Educate them for peace, harmony, but this will only be achieved when they are guaranteed the security, support and protection they deserve as a child.

EDUCATING FOR PEACE

There is really no manual that has a recipe for parents and guardians giving them guidelines on how to educate their children so that they can do well in life, in their personal development and in society, if there is one, it is difficult to do it to the letter. It is likely that if someone wanted to put it into practice, however, it would not have the expected result because children receive information from both the home and the outside world. In such a case, a manual should be written for everyone, but without results because each household as a single society has its own rules, and different ways of raising and educating their children are dealt with.

Parents educate their children in the best way they have learned from their parents and according to their education or that of their ancestors, their culture and the society in which they live. When they are children, most follow the rules, but when they reach adolescence they let themselves be carried away by peer pressure. They listen more to what their classmates or friends say, so much so that some teens don't want other friends watching them walking around with their parents all the time, or that they are constantly at school talking to the teacher. Situation that could create some confusion or kind of discouragement in certain parents, some do not know what to do. Others feel confused and helpless; educating their children is something that is unique to each family, and highly personal to parents and society in general. However, even though each family individually has a pattern for the formation of their children and gives them quite a lot of results. It is possible that the same rule will not result in another home. Because children are not only influenced by parents, they are also bombarded with information from the outside world.

From school-age friends, television and most of the media. Eventually, if there is not adequate supervision by adults, it could be that children are getting much more than they should, depending on their age. All of these will have repercussions on the way they behave, no matter how diligent the parents and guardians are in their training. Although there are no established rules regarding the education of children and adolescents. If we want our children and adolescents to grow up as less violent and aggressive men and women who can live in society without being harmed. And that they do no harm to other people, we must begin to create strategies, look for resources, build new tools, aimed at training our children, free of abuse, aggression and harassment.

It is time to lay the foundation stone in the first place where they begin to socialize, to develop. It should be the most propitious place where they should feel safe and confident, respected, protected and loved, the home, their home.

There in their family environment, where they were received. In any other home, they may have had to live in, even if they have no blood ties. The best way to educate children is with love and respect, children and adolescents who receive understanding, support, security in their homes, who can express themselves freely. They are children, who will not be bullying any other children. Every child who is respected learns to show respect. The main place to start with bullying prevention is at home. Although the development of their personality will depend on internal and external factors, as each is different, unique and unrepeatable. They are learning from what they observe at home, from their family environment more than anywhere else. Household education will be a determining factor in their personal development, it is very likely that those households where there is an environment of tolerance, children will learn to be tolerant. If effective communication is encouraged that they can express themselves without being punished or censored. Being fair is learned in an environment of justice and only when they are respected will they learn to respect others. If children feel insecure, abused, offended and violated in any way, if they are treated with hostility. This feeling of anguish generates sadness and resentment in them, this same feeling of anguish is projected outwards and towards the other children. If that situation is not corrected, they will have those roots when they reach adulthood, become abusive, hostile, spiteful people, the children, who are mistreated, who grow up watching the violence in their homes, will believe that all these misbehaviors are normal. This is how they will treat other children, both at school and in their own environment. In the event that they do not receive adequate treatment at an early age, such unmodified behavior is much more likely to continue into adulthood. If we want the Bullying to stop, to disappear, we must all create solidity, valid and lasting strategies, in the short and long term. This is not a school problem, it's where it spreads, nests in school. They originate in another place and space, not all children, and adolescents who behave violently. Most of them have good manners and good behavior. Almost all people have different concepts from what values are, but in a general sense most human values are universal.

That society or country would not appreciate that its citizens are people who respect the laws, the property of others and people. If we educate children, to be respectful, this is achieved only by starting to treat them with respect. Only in this way they learn to respect the rights of others, part of this respect includes not bullying another child. Prevention plays an important role. Even to prevent a physical or mental illness from spreading, the best solution would be to prevent it. How to prevent bullying in schools. It is not as simple as it seems because in a school there are children, with different customs and cultures. Each one has brought with them a series of experiences according to what they have lived and learned from the environment in which they have developed. Without leaving aside internal factors that belong to each individual individually. Children do not only learn from their parents in this modern world in which we live, there is a great bombardment of information to which they are exposed.

Even if you want to, it becomes very difficult to control. There is another problem is that parents do not have the time to be at home supervising the children, at all times, the many occupations of today has made it difficult enough for parents to offer their children a great deal of time. But how about if you start with a little quality, not everything is lost, that they feel important, dear, loved, appreciated, when they need correction don't yell at them. Whether they are disciplined with love, effective dialogue offers greater results than fighting or yelling, lawsuits and shouting only make children anxious, nervous, rebellious and disobedient. In order to shout out what he can say in a quiet voice, even the children will understand that they are being corrected for their own good. It is not advisable to have a discussion with the youngsters, unless it is not to discuss a healthy, violence-free, non-controversial topic; if you discipline it in the presence of your siblings, your little friends or other people you will only get the children. And above all, adolescents lose respect for the people who are shouting at them. When parents are tolerant, they will copy, recording that information in their small brains, when they reach adulthood there is a greater probability. Let them be tolerant of even their own parents, they will teach the next generations. Teach them fellowship by example, without aggression of any kind, solidarity, friendship, honesty, loyalty, when children live in homes where adults are criticized they will learn to criticize. And as a general rule, future generations could become people who will repeat this behavior. Parents are not being burdened with too much responsibility. In order to reduce this

Bullying problem, it is simply that when children and adolescents are treated with respect and dignity. Teach them to respect, starting by respecting their rights to be children and adolescents, that they can have comfort in their home, freedom. It's not that they let themselves go out on the streets or walk around without their parents' permission, that's not what freedom is all about, it's that they can enjoy their childhood without censorship. Free from offenses and not being robbed of their right to be children. When they have a problem at school, on the streets or in any place, they are able to seek understanding from their parents or guardians without fear of screaming or abuse. Good work is needed in both homes and schools to provide space. Places free of hostility, comfortable homes, schools that provide security, protection and well-being for as long as they remain on campus. Give them a world full of peace.

A better society for the next generations, regardless of whether they are our children or not, where children and adolescents feel free, happy and at ease. Make sure they're safe and satisfied. That they can grow physically and mentally healthy.

When someone tries to bully them, they are so emotionally strong that teasing and bullying doesn't affect them in the least bit, that they are able to talk to their teachers and especially parents. There has always been bullying, although little attention has been paid to it, perhaps because the situation was not as serious as it is today. This bombardment of words aimed at hurting and hurting, damaging the esteem, character and personality of children and adolescents. Sorry, this doesn't start in schools, it's in some houses, therefore. It is at home that we must begin to lay the groundwork for bullying at school. This problem is not of today has always been said to be present, but it has not taken so much, although we have seen alarming numbers of boys and girls who drop out of school for fear of being bullied. Young people who, while it is true that they have not attempted an attempt on their lives or that of another schoolmate, have become emotionally incapacitated, their personality has been destroyed. This can stop if everyone in charge of the children begins to become aware. The solution for this has its roots primarily in homes, schools and society itself.

First parents training their children with a quality education, no quantity is required. As has already been said in previous chapters, an education based on values with examples, educating, disciplining is not offending or mistreating, it is not necessary to raise the tone of voice. An affable treatment achieves wonders, love speaking even to the hearts of stone and the Heart of children, is very sensitive to good treatment, to affections. Discipline is not synonymous with offenses and words that are wrong and inadequate, it must be offered an education for the future for the next generations, educating to form people useful to society. to reduce violence. They deserve to live in peace. This can only be achieved without violence, promoting education in the home based on a rich communication. that there is responsibility. No child will learn to be responsible if he or she begins to carry homework to school without doing so. They will not be punctual if they do not comply with school schedules or observe that these rules of schedules are violated by those who must show responsibility for them to assimilate a correct behavior of commitments. Homework and chores left by teachers must be done by children, adolescents and supervised by their parents and guardians before they take it to school. No child is born honest, not supportive to the established principles and norms, they will learn and put them into practice in the same way that they observe that older people do. If you preach one thing to them and they see that adults do another, it will only create an ambivalence in their personality because they will not know what to abstain from. The best recipe for teaching children is by example. They look, observe, assimilate, analyze and draw their own conclusions. As long as parents devote more attention to children and adolescents, without harassment or persecution, they will have a greater part of the road traveled than in the future. Parents have more peace of mind, less headaches, of course, it is clear that it is necessary to see who the friendships of their children are, all this will influence the way they behave. Some parents and guardians devote all their time and energy to ensuring that their sons and daughters are well-behaved men and women, but if we do not watch out for who they meet, both in and out of school, it is likely that all this effort and sacrifice will not produce any results because bad company is also a factor to consider, if there is no good foundation. As parents, you have to be aware of everything about your children. Teachers play a very important role in the school and could contribute when indicators of bullying and violence appear. Without the cooperation of parents and guardians, there is nothing the school can do, even if they make the most of their best efforts, in working together where they should be involved. Parents, guardians, the school and when things get out of control to some sector of the community. The school is responsible for developing educational programs for the purpose of identifying. And decrease violence, talks, conversations, and everything that contributes to maintain peace and harmony among students. Especially aimed at preventing and stopping bullying in schools.

It is an arduous, constant, and perhaps a difficult job for some, but if we want to form better generations it is time to start at home and of course in all the schools, offering more vigilance, while the boys are in school, all the teaching staff is responsible for those children, and adolescents who are inside. The greater the supervision, the less violence, the clearer the rules serve as protection for the future men and women of society. At home, it is the responsibility of the

children's family and adolescents in the schools of the teaching staff. When parents, tutors and teachers work together,
we will surely be creating a better world for the men and women of tomorrow. It is important to create possible solutions
to detect, combat bullying outbreaks, not the perpetrator
they have a behavior that in time can change. It's not fighting the boys, girls and adolescents who bully. Rather, it is to
create the bases in homes, schools and society so that these
conditions do not appear, which provoke and produce the
outbreaks of violence and aggression in children. The teens
that bully, also need help. Some of them drag some situation
or conflict that they can't channel; the levels of violence,
bullying will only be reduced when there are no children
who are abused, mistreated, sad, bitter, wounded, stressed,
distressed, distressed, desperate, malnourished, undernouri-
shed, homeless, not because they have been abandoned, but
because the attention. Affection and supervision is very poor,
when a good esteem and a strong enough mind is fostered in
the minors, even if they are mocked or mocked. However,
even so, when good work is done in the search to eradicate
bullying, it is most likely that from time to time there will
spring up small roots, because children could be educated
in their family environment. However, it must be taken into
account that society does not consist of a single home, there
are millions of homes. The world is made up of many individuals, everyone has a different way of looking at the things
of life and it is something that must be respected. It is up to
each household to create firm and solid tools for when these unwanted outbreaks appear children and adolescents do
not feel so vulnerable, everywhere there will be everything,
the serious recommendable thing. To create strong estimates
and minds in the minors so that they end up affected as little
as possible when problems arise. Perhaps it is not possible to
free him from the difficulties that life brings and daily life,
there are many things that the human being is not an act to
control, even if he could not want.

Communication, the dialogue of parents and guardians with minors is part of the tools to take into account. An environment of peace, trust, harmony and all that has been said above is needed for children to be able to live in a changing and globalized world, but to find wellbeing and security wherever they are. Even more so when it comes to their home and second home, school. The best and most effective strategy to prevent bullying and other ramifications, will always be an education rich in values, homes full of peace, love and respect. Without prejudice to the security that must prevail on school grounds.

BULLYING: HOW TO TREAT AND PREVENT IT

Preventing bullying could become a challenge, especially when it comes to school bullying. First it would be necessary to identify the possible causes that lead a child or teenager to annoy one or other classmates in their classroom or school. If we start from the point of view that it is not a single cause that produces aggression in children and adolescents, with the knowledge that influences multi-factorial, biological, cultural and social reasons and that the environment in which minors operate, really influence their way of behaving. Taking into account that the circumstances of each individual, are very different from those of others. First, we must focus on the roots that encourage and become triggers of violence; we must go beyond the appearances that seem to be the causes that make children and adolescents aggressive, to such a high degree that it is transformed into ridicule or psychological or physical mistreatment towards one or another classmate or schoolmate. Bullying, which the victim receives by causing suffering, pain and anguish for a perpetrator, whether child or adolescent, can be a somewhat complicated matter, a bullying child, undoubtedly going through some internal or external situation that pushes him to move towards his victim.

In order to prevent bullying, we must start by making society aware that this has become a problem that not only diminishes the victim's self-esteem, destroys his or her personality, and even destroys his or her life. The first thing is that it should be recognized as a problem that leaves human losses. Anything that weakens thinking ability, leads to discouragement, causing anxiety, depression, suffering and pain in someone must be immediately and effectively addressed.

Everyone as a society can unite to work together, if we want a better society with healthy women and men with their minds, living in harmony with all other living beings, we need to make a restructuring both in society and in the family environment, where children and adolescents have their first experiences of life, with adults who receive them for the first time since they leave their mothers' womb until they reach adulthood. Although it is recognized that there are many factors that can turn a child or adolescent into a victimizer, home education plays without a doubt the most important role, a good foundation in terms of family education, serves as a basis for when they have to face the outside world Family education is a good platform, which allows them to be able to deal with a lot of information, which they will learn outside the home, but will also encounter different situations to which they will be ready. Facilitating them with a strong and healthy mind, they will be able to overcome the obstacles and problems that arise along the way during their development. And to be able to handle all those ranges of problems that one way or another arrive. One of them could be the ghost of bullying when they arrive at school, who are able to communicate with adults from the very beginning of the first rates of aggression. Observation will always be advisable for children, some do not talk about something that is happening to them, but they could have repetitive behavior, especially the youngest ones, related to what has happened in school or elsewhere. In order to prevent levels of violence in children and adolescents, adult participation is crucial. Even if there are no outbreaks of violence in a home, exposure to subliminal television programs and some violent video gameplay can become factors that cause behavior change in a child more than in others, even when they live with peaceful individuals. Preventing school bullying is not just an issue that falls solely on parents, although it is the adult of the home who is responsible for laying the main foundation, offering the child a home where there is an atmosphere of peace, harmony, understanding, unconditional support, protection, caring for both their physical and emotional development, so that their self-esteem is kept in balance, and adding all the necessary elements that a child requires to grow as an individual, that log The school gets its share of the investment, because children spend a short or long period of time there. While in school, it must provide not only a comprehensive quality academic education, but also continuous supervision of the children in their care during that period of time. The school must ensure the protection and safety of children while in school. It is up to the school to create tools that are valid and robust enough to maintain safety and quiet on campus. And it is up to the teacher to innovate strategies so that students are calm, attentive, and focused, while teaching the precious bread of teaching; when one of the students is distracted within the classroom; there is a great likelihood that others will fall into the same. Without getting to the rigidity the teacher should maintain control, in the classroom, clear rules in front of the bullying spotlights, could be favorable, once the first Bullying indicator is presented, should be stopped, parents should be involved in everything that has to do with their children. And of course, school administrators should also be informed of any classroom situations that arise. If bullying is recognized as a social problem, which affects us in one way or another as a society, then it is time for all of us to come together to work towards its prevention. And so that both the victim and the perpetrator are offered good treatment; psychological therapies that must be provided by a trained, trained and authorized professional to carry out this type of treatment. The prevention of school bullying must be timely, without letting its roots grow and before its branches stop at school. Encourage true communication in the home, peace, security, love, respect, that children are taught their homework as they grow up. But that their rights are equally respected, the corrections to minors must be free of aggression, that there is no violence of any kind, emotional, psychological, physical, or any other kind. In order to prevent bullying at school, the levels of violence between adults responsible for children and all those living with them in the same household should be reduced.

Children should receive unconditional support from parents and guardians both emotionally and academically. Adult supervision is a very important axis, knowing who your children's friends are, what they do in their company and where they go. Good supervision and monitoring of the programs that children watch on TV, and especially when they are teenagers who watch and watch on social networks. It's not right to let children have access to all the information on social networks, it doesn't mean that they are going to be away from technology, on the contrary, they must grow with technological advances. All this helps them to develop their intellectual capacity, allows them a great breadth of knowledge and helps them to carry out their schoolwork. All of this is beneficial and helpful as long as there is adult supervision. Technology in addition to helping them to fulfill their academic duties offers them the opportunity to discover their talents, expand their intellectual abilities. Allowing them to keep up with the modern world. Children who have access to technology have a better chance of developing the maximum skills and intellectual abilities in relation to those who do not have it, who may be at a disadvantage. Supervision is of vital importance. If we have the intention and wish to prevent school bullying, we need to encourage a solid family education based on values.

It is very likely that each society has a different concept of what values are, but everyone would like to have people who are kind, respectful, honest, honest, caring, responsible and sensitive.

In order to prevent bullying in schools, it is necessary that the levels of verbal psychological violence and all the indicators that could provoke any type of aggression or violence are lowered in the home. In a special way to avoid the physical and psychological mistreatment that some relatives do to children and adolescents. Anything that can contribute to the prevention of bullying in schools will be extremely important. However, it is necessary for society to take part, look at and approach Bullying as a problem that has been affecting our children and young people for a long time. Many children between the ages of ten and fourteen have suffered from bullying at school or on their cell phones, and when it comes to teenagers between the ages of fourteen and seventeen, the number is alarming. Some do the Bullying personally, through a telephone and others use social networks. If we all stand up as a society to work together as one body. Together in search of solutions, aimed at preventing bullying in schools, there will come a time when we will not have to worry, because there will no longer be any more child victims or perpetrators.

Rather, it is to create the bases in homes, schools and society so that these conditions do not appear, which provoke and produce the outbreaks of violence and aggression in minors.

The role of the family is to provide them with homes where values are present and where they must be filled with peace, tranquility, and love. So that there is no lack of affection in children, they do not experience any kind of emptiness inside them, since lack of affection could become a trigger.

Create communication channels in the home for children and adolescents to talk to their parents, guardians when they are being bullied or bullied by one of their classmates in the classroom or school. The role of the elders must be to listen to them, from the first moment they want to speak.

Support them at all times, motivate them to face problems with diplomacy, using dialogue as a good way to resolve conflicts. Violence can only be combated with education, that is and always will be the main key to control and prevent bullying in schools. However, children need love and understanding from all their loved ones; they need to feel loved, supported, accepted and understood.

Even if there are sanctions and many more drastic ones are created, applicable against those who bully, however severe the sanctions may be. These will not help to stop this problem that affects us so much. We do nothing if society is not made aware of the need to work on family restructuring. Putting controls on everything that produces violence, to which children and adolescents are exposed every day.

Sanctions against perpetrators will have no effect unless the bases are created to eliminate the indicators produced by the sources of violence and verbal, non-verbal, physical and psychological aggression. An action plan is needed, aimed at the design of educational programs, in order to educate the first family society, so that they in turn contribute to reducing levels of domestic violence. Until there is no change in the way children are educated, it will be very difficult for bullying to decrease or be prevented. Nor will this behavior be eliminated by combating the perpetrator, they are children and adolescents who need to be treated with an effective psychological treatment. Education is a good tool for combating violence, if we educate our children today there will be no need to imprison adults tomorrow. Although school bullying appears in school, we must create awareness that its roots are not born there. The seed that Bullying produces is in some homes and in society itself. For this reason, it is incumbent on all of us as a society to fight for solutions to this problem.

We all have the voice and power to change the world of our children and adolescents, educating them with love, is the only way to transform people. Then let us educate children with values, and especially with love for them, for humanity and for living beings. Both the victim and the offender require that they be offered treatment. With follow-up, it is not a transitory matter, of a day, a behavior does not change overnight, taking into account that each one of the problems of each individual, is different and must be treated according to the situation and circumstances that cause it, in a particular way. The victim as a victim and the perpetrator as such, since some emptiness inside or outside the victim is motivating him/her to annoy another child. It is very true that all of us as a society have the duty to offer our childhood a world full of harmony of peace and love, and that the first to lay the foundation stone are the homes, the family.

Bullying prevention must start at home, with zero violence towards children, and in front of them. However, we can all prevent bullying at school.

With the same intensity as a series of existing problems. It's time to start seeing Bullying as a problem that causes pain and suffering in the victim and ultimately ends her life. Knowing that there is a great deal of information from the outside world to which they are exposed, regardless of the good work parents are doing. The society itself must be involved, so that effective work is achieved for its prevention.

Families in particular can work in this sense, supporting and supervising them, because the Bullying itself does not arise alone. Behind it there are a series of factors that provoke it, to investigate the causes why boys attack others. Once we have identified its origin in an exhaustive manner, work together between the school and the family. It is always necessary to let both the victim and the perpetrator know how important they are to their family. And equally for school and above all for society, that the minors recognize that they are the future, without them our society would become extinct.

To maintain a true and effective communication with children from an early age, so that when they reach adolescence they have confidence in their parents to tell them everything that is happening inside their little head, their mind, in school or outside it.

Create homes that offer an environment of peace, security, and harmony where they feel supported, loved and protected.

To strengthen the self-esteem of children and adolescents, at all times and circumstances, so that they can face any Bullying or other problems.

Keep watchfulness and control of children's television and social networking programs.

Lower levels of violence in the family environment and all types of physical, psychological, and emotional violence.

Educate children with a good family education based on values: tolerance, companionship, solidarity, cooperation, humility, responsibility, and respect.

Talk to children and adolescents about bullying, emphasizing the harm it causes to the victim and its consequences for the victim. Explain the suffering the victim has to go through. Above all, when they are teenagers, they do not measure their actions, they only act without thinking about consequences. They must be presented with the dangers that the victim runs in the short and long term, that this Bullying behavior is not correct, and therefore the offender will have to pay in some way for his or her action.

Encourage children to resolve conflicts based on dialogue, free of violence.

Some quality time must be given to children so that they do not feel alone and unprotected. That there are no spaces in them to feel alone and abandoned as much as possible, the food they receive should be rich in nutrients, a balanced diet allows them to develop well both physically and emotionally. All the contribution that parents can make to keeping children in good manners inside and outside their homes is favorable. However, it is up to the school to cooperate effectively so that parents' work does not end up in a vacuum.

Design strategies at the school level to identify the first Bullying hotspots, once they occur, develop formulas to stop it before it contaminates more students. Otherwise the situation could become uncontrollable. With the first indicator of violence from one student to another, whether classroom or campus, parents or guardians of minors should be informed. Stopping bullying will prevent it from spreading throughout the classroom and the school itself, so it is up to the teacher to be alert. Once he realizes that a child begins with subtle words against one of his peers, he must find appropriate ways to stop it and not allow it to spread throughout the classroom.

Include bullying in the academic curriculum, as a topic to be addressed to teach children and adolescents from the very first years that they should not make fun of other children and educate them with a no, no to violence. Let them know how much harm and suffering it does to the victim and the possible consequences for the perpetrator.

To make students aware that bullying is a serious problem that can destroy the esteem of others and even lead them to make drastic and regrettable decisions that could extend beyond school, affecting the family and society.

Students should recognize that bullying is destructive, that it can destroy the lives and dreams of individuals. That a simple, innocent mockery or intimidation can become a destructive weapon so potent that it is capable of destroying personality, character and self-esteem and ending the person's life.

Teachers are responsible for creating strategies within the classroom so that no child or adolescent ends up being bullied. As far as possible, create living environments and good relationships between students, both in the classroom and at school.

It will always be the school's responsibility to maintain the safety and security of students while they remain in the school.

For this reason, the first Bullying indicator should work to stop this inappropriate behavior, always with the participation of parents.

It is necessary to include in the academic curriculum a subject on education in values, starting from the first levels. For students to learn, from an early age the value of the person, and how to live in society without having to make fun of others. That they know how to live in a world where we are all different, even though we are equal as human beings, but that everyone without exception deserves respect, regardless of their condition, creed, race, or color, age, or any other situation, or circumstances that they may be going through. That the children and adolescents receive talks and conversations by trained personnel on self-esteem, companionship, tolerance and solidarity. All this aimed at fostering and strengthening coexistence and harmony among students, they learn to respect the ways others think, knowing that each is unique and different. It could be helpful to dramatize with the students some facts where someone has been a victim of Bullying. Focusing on the pain and suffering of the victim and also the consequences and sanctions for the perpetrator.

It is the school's role to develop prevention programs aimed at preventing the spread of all types of aggression, with bullying in school as a priority.

A good rapprochement between the family and the educational community serves as a basis to prevent the spread of bullying. A greater communication between parents and school, will not only serve to prevent bullying outbreaks, it also contributes to better academic performance and good behavior of the students being this way all parties will benefit, school, students and of course the parents will ultimately get the best quota.

Society can also get involved by placing its small grain of sand, to prevent, stop and eradicate bullying in schools, because we know that bullying, although ends up in school, it has been transformed into a social problem, which is wiping out our children and adolescents.

Community centers could contribute by implementing educational programs through the means at their disposal to help parents who do not know how to deal with this problem when their children become victims or perpetrators.

Let's all work together to prevent bullying at school. Let us remember that the best way to educate children and adolescents is with love and respect, giving them their rights and of course teaching them their duties. When we all work with the same feelings, parents, school and society, all united, searching for tools and resources with the aim of avoiding that minors are exposed to any kind of violence or aggression, we will be walking along a safe path, free from bullying. It is necessary to work with families, because the factors that influence the emergence of bullying outbreaks are, multi-factorial, so many biological, cultural and social factors, influence for children and adolescents to present these behaviors. In order to deal with bullying, it is necessary to take into account each of the factors that could become triggers. Once we have identified them, it will be necessary to work with each of them individually, to draw lines and create solid foundations, aimed at prevention, treatment, and elimination. Until we work with the elements that produce it, our fight against bullying will be more difficult, if not impossible. The impossible ones do not exist, if you want to achieve something, even if you have to do a hard work and join forces. In this case of bullying, it is necessary to unite everyone as if every child and adolescent belongs to our family in particular, all of them are part of our society.

Once the possible triggers are identified, we will necessarily have to join forces. Since it is not a problem of school, it concerns all of us as a society to form children and adolescents with a good character and balanced personality. Remembering that when one of them achieves a great achievement we all rejoice, but in the same way when another presents an inappropriate behavior, we all end up paying a high price. For this reason, therefore, let us raise, in the same spirit, with one voice, to provide a better society for the future men and women of tomorrow.

We could create strategies aimed at providing teachers with good training so that when the first bullying indicator is presented in their classroom, they are prepared to handle it before it spreads throughout the school.

Create centers where parents can find help to help both the victim and the perpetrator. And at the same time to guide parents about the best way to treat their child who is a

Bullying victim and/or the perpetrator. Another positive tool would be to create a school for parents to help them with any problems concerning their children. All this must be carried out by trained, authorized and trained personnel. The most powerful weapon to end violence will undoubtedly always be education.

Knowing that true education doesn't necessarily come from school, it has its roots at home.

CONCLUSION

The aim of this book is not to teach parents and guardians how to educate their children. Much less to give them a recipe to apply it; nothing like that. Under no circumstances, even if there was a manual, and there are thousands of books that show them the most appropriate way to be parents; or how to raise good and better children; upright citizens, free of prejudices, with good character, emotionally healthy, physically and psychologically, adept and useful to participate in society. Men and women who are dignified and prosperous, honest, tolerant, supportive, peaceful; there will always be variables that people cannot control. Over time, many parents have taken great care to educate their children in the right way and some things are out of their hands. Respecting a family's right to raise their child. The sole purpose of this work is to contribute a grain of sand from the millions that are on the shore of the sea. Trying to create sustainable, long-lasting tools in the search for solutions to prevent, and stop bullying school. Not only in schools, which seem to be the place of origin, but undoubtedly, bullying transcends beyond that. The roots are not in schools, although it is usually in them that the problem tends to explode. Bullying is gradually originating in households, as well as certain external variables which parents would never be able to control. This book is the result of a long experience working with children and adolescents in different public and private schools. It stems from the helplessness, pain, sadness, despair and suffering caused by seeing countless children and young adults who are victims of Bullying; psychologically destroyed, with their feelings wounded, emotionally scarred, and physically injured. It is not easy to look at a young person bleeding on the outside, knowing that they are torn inside. Even if the wounds are not perceived, they are there, latent inside their being, destroying their self-esteem and personality. Knowing some have died because of Bullying.

Knowing that Bullying is not only present at school, it has roots, deeper roots. It is like a big tree that its branch spreads through many places and spaces. It goes beyond the schools. The only purpose is to seek an awakening in society so that bullying school is approached as a major problem that causes suffering to our children and adolescents and, of course, to their families. All of us as a society can join forces, work, think about all the positive contributions we can make and innovate others to stop violence against children and adolescents. And among them, build tools and use all available resources to stop bullying in schools; develop strategies so that, as much as possible, children can live in favorable environments; homes where they feel wanted, loved, supported, allowed to be what they are - children-, free from any kind of abuse, or violence. Make sure they are offered quality time. Although it is not possible to give quantity, they do not require quantity, they want to feel secure. They want to feel as though their rights are not violated - they are taught their duties, but without any focus on violence or aggression. Real homes where they feel free to express their feelings, their concerns, to say no, when necessary. Where communication is present at all times, let them be told the truth. May peace, harmony, cooperation, solidarity, fellowship, tolerance, understanding, love and respect be fostered. A family education based on values far from detrimental, will allow both children and adolescents to respect diversity while promoting coexistence in society. All, parents, schools, society as a whole, in the search for solutions, create awareness to prevent, stop, avoid, treat, and of course eradicate Bullying. All united as a society to stop bullying school. It is time to look at it as the problem it is. One that harms the victim, causes emotional suffering and brings consequences that are detrimental to the perpetrator.

Made in the USA
Lexington, KY
13 November 2019